W9-CHV-343

EDUCATIONAL IMAGERY

EDUCATIONAL
IMAGERY

Strategies to Personalize
Classroom Instruction

By

GLENN E. RICHARDSON, Ph.D.

College of Education
Texas A&M University
College Station, Texas

CHARLES   C   THOMAS   •   PUBLISHER
Springfield • Illinois • U.S.A.

Published and Distributed Throughout the World by

CHARLES C THOMAS • PUBLISHER

2600 South First Street

Springfield, Illinois 62717, U.S.A.

© 1982 *by* CHARLES C THOMAS • PUBLISHER

ISBN 0-398-04639-5

Library of Congress Catalog Card Number 81-16698

*With THOMAS BOOKS careful attention is given to all details of
manufacturing and design. It is the Publisher's desire to present books that are
satisfactory as to their physical qualities and artistic possibilities and
appropriate for their particular use. THOMAS BOOKS will be true to those
laws of quality that assure a good name and good will.*

Printed in the United States of America

I-RX-1

Library of Congress Cataloging in Publication Data

Richardson, Glenn E.
    Educational imagery.

    Bibliography: p.
    Includes index.
    1. Learning, Psychology of.   2. Imagery
(Psychology)   3. Imagination.   4. Teaching.   I. Title.
LB1051.R5143   370.15'23   81-16698
ISBN 0-398-04639-5   AACR2

*to Glenwood and Ruth
for solid foundations*

*to Kathleen
for joy in the present*

*to Brannon and Tavan
for hope and confidence in the future*

PREFACE

The classroom instructional method of educational imagery has taken three years to development, which, generally speaking, has been the process of applying basic principles of counseling, psychotherapy, and decision making to classroom instruction. The method has application and potential productivity for all areas of the education curriculum. Even though the focus in this book tends toward the social studies, health, and contemporary student dilemmas and issues, examples and suggestions toward the sciences, English and the arts are included. Groups that have found the method effective and productive have been as young as first and second grade children in elementary school and as seasoned as adult learners and veteran teachers. Because of professional interest and expertise, most of the strategies presented in this book are geared toward secondary and university students, although Chapter 9 focuses on educational imagery and the elementary school student.

Educational imagery is very diversified in that the strategy can last as long as thirty seconds or thirty minutes depending on the function and nature of the strategy. Strategies have been fun, happy, positive, and recreational as well as emotionally draining and difficult decision-making experiences. Groups that have had positive responses to the strategy have been conservative, liberal, and mixed. The method of presentation has ranged from students being asked to take a few seconds to imagine a selected cognitive problem, to situations in which students have been asked to lie down on the floor, go through relaxation strategies, and spend twenty minutes working out difficult emotional dilemmas. In summary, the method of educational imagery has been tried in almost every situation in the public school system with most types of groups and with many different functions, and the recommendations made in this book are those which have proven most successful without controversy.

Subjective evaluations by students even in the initial stages of development have been so positive that the author was motivated and excited about refining the method. Several studies are now being conducted to measure objectively the efficacy of educational imagery as a method in terms of cognitive gains, affective shifts, and behavioral outcomes, but the results of those reports are beyond the scope of this book. The purpose here is to describe educational imagery in such a way that the reader will be able to incorporate the strategy into his or her methodological arsenal. In the meantime until those studies are reported, it is safe to assume, based on the preliminary findings, that educational imagery is not only an interesting break in traditional methods but also a boon to the educational process.

The fast emerging concept of imagery and now its application in the classroom may be the most innovative educational method since values clarification because it continues to include the relevancy of affective dimension yet adds more individuality and also functions in the cognitive and behavior dimension of education. I hope the reader will benefit from this book not only because of the ideas and structures that are presented herein but also to trigger his or her imagination and creativity to develop strategies in his/her own areas of interest and expertise.

CONTENTS

LIST OF
EDUCATIONAL IMAGERY STRATEGIES

EDUCATIONAL
IMAGERY

Chapter 1

EDUCATIONAL IMAGERY:
THE CONCEPT

How can I provide my students with an atmosphere that will allow them to make productive, informed, "in class" decisions without the influence of their peers?

How can I individualize and personalize instruction in large classes?

With such a variance in values, attitudes, and behaviors among my students, how can I deal with sensitive topic areas without offending someone?

Is there some innovative method to reinforce cognitive information without boring the students?

The spiritual dimension of issues is becoming popular, but how should I deal with it without bias and respect individual backgrounds?

How can I effectively bridge the gap between having the students make good decisions and performing them?

These kinds of questions exemplify the concern that caring teachers are demonstrating in the pursuit of more humanistic, individualized, personalized, and effective teaching methods. It is in the spirit of these questions and many others that the concept of educational imagery was developed.

THE CONCEPT

The concept of imagery is not new but is a tried and true method in counseling, psychotherapy, and physical education. The innovation that is emerging in education is applying the method and concept of imagery into the classroom setting. Educational imagery is a classroom method that allows the students to isolate themselves mentally and to use their natural abilities to daydream or fantasize in ways that accomplish educational objectives. Educational imagery is used in facilitating decision making, clarifying values, memorizing, incorporating behavioral outcomes of teaching, reinforcing cognitive concepts, and other functions that will be described later in the book. The teacher directs the process by describing scenarios that the students imagine as clearly as they can using the imaginary senses of seeing, hearing, touching, smelling and tasting. The scenario is designed by the teacher to accomplish one of the several functions described in this chapter, such as leading the students into a nonoffensive decision-making scenario in which they make choices based on acquired information and personal values. Another option may be for the teacher to lead the students completely through a scenario to reinforce a cognitive concept.

To clarify, any topic that has a behavioral implication, that is something that can change the student's life-style for the good, has potential for an educational imagery strategy. The application or decision making occurs as the students contemplate the behavior and the teacher introduces the strategy by saying something like the following: "We are going to do something today. I would like you to get comfortable by sitting up straight and letting your head just relax on your shoulders." After dimming the lights (although not on the first time in most cases), the teacher guides the students through a brief relaxation exercise that isolates the students mentally. (examples of a relaxation strategy are given in Chapter 3). The instructor then describes a situation relevant to the behavioral topic with which all the students can identify, describing environments such as "their home," a "favorite place to eat," "after school going home," and related to people they can identify such as "a good friend," "a parent or guardian," and other general terminology that conjures individualized scenarios.

The students are encouraged to visualize the surroundings with all the colors, shapes, movements, sounds, smells, touch, and other sensory action when appropriate in the scenario. If the purpose of the strategy is to make a decision regarding a particular behavior, then the teacher guides the students into a decision-making scenario related to that selected behavior. For example, if the behavioral outcome is for the student to decide to smoke or not to smoke cigarettes, then a scene could be developed by the instructor that would place the student in a "favorite place" with a good friend with the friend offering a cigarette to the student. The teacher would leave the remainder of the scenario (whether the student smokes or not) to be completed by the students and allows time and silence for the student to do so. Whether the student had been a regular smoker or only on an experimental basis, following a unit on smoking, then students will have the opportunity to make a choice regarding smoking in light of new information. The appropriate time in the unit plan would seem to be following the information about the consequences of smoking, the clarification of values, and perhaps discussion on how to say no to a friend and still maintain friendships or "be cool." The other variations and scenarios, as will be demonstrated in later chapters, range from choosing foods to safety in shop classes.

It is unfortunate that fantasizing and daydreaming have generally negative connotations in society. When one daydreams in class, the student is labeled as an inattentive student and offends the classroom teacher who is trying to capture the interest of students related to a topic area. Daydreaming or fantasizing is a powerful human quality that inables a person to visualize far away places, hear sounds that cannot be brought into the classroom, and plunge into situations that may or may not ever occur in real life. This powerful ability to imagine seems to lie dormant in educational methodology and unfortunately continues to carry the stigma of a negative behavior rather than channeling this human quality into a powerful, exciting, and meaningful teaching tool. How often do teachers struggle to keep the student's mind on what he/she is saying for fifty or sixty minutes when the attention span of students generally does not approach near that length of time? When we do lose their attention, what happens?

They daydream. Again, why not capture that imagination and help the student in one of several functions using the daydreaming as the teaching method.

There are as many potential functions of educational imagery as there are teaching approaches and probably more when a creative mind grasps its concept and potential. The following sections describe some of the developed functions.

COGNITIVE IMAGERY

For the teacher who deals basically in the cognitive realm and for those who supplement the cognitive with affective and behavioral methods, educational imagery can serve three functions to foster cognitive learning. The functions are to prepare or "ready" students to learn the material, to aid in learning, and to reinforce the cognitive information and concepts.

The first function is labeled *readiness imagery* and functions to prepare students to receive the information that the teacher has prepared. For example, in English literature, a readiness imagery strategy could be prepared that would set the mood for a poem, short story, or novel, typifying conditions of the times of the writing of the work or of the setting. In history courses, the same readiness strategy would prepare the students to study a battle, debate, bill, or a law by mentally putting the students into that time in history and relating the events leading up to the point of study. In mathematics, through educational imagery, the students could imagine a problem that needed to be solved but would be difficult to solve with the students' current level of math. Recognizing the need, the new instruction on how to solve the problem would make the new information more meaningful.

The second form of cognitive imagery is to help in the learning process itself. There has been a substantial amount of research indicating that learning words and lists of words, is facilitated when the words carry natural images (such as *wagon, run, green,* etc.) in contrast to those that do not (such as *vague, slight, easy,* etc.). The implication and function of cognitive imagery are to encourage the memorization of vocabulary words and meanings by developing cognitive imagery strategies that create images in the minds of students to aid in the memorization process. In mathematics, when a word, addition, subtraction, or geometrical problem needs to be solved, it will be remembered more readily if a cognitive imagery causes relationship images in the minds of students.

The third function of educational imagery as a cognitive function is entitled *cognitive reinforcing imagery*. The importance of review and repeating information for short- and long-term memory is clear and important to assure that students have grasped concepts and information. Rather than repeating the concepts in a lecture sense, educational imagery, in a creative way, could reinforce the cognitive information. For example, if the students had just completed a study of the circulatory system in biology or physiology, the students could imagine taking a "fantastic voyage" and shrink in a capsule, mentally of course, and take a ride through the circulatory system. If the elementary science students had learned about the water cycle, they could visualize the cycle as they become a drop of water and experience the cycle.

AFFECTIVE IMAGERY

In the last few years, teachers have expanded the dimensions of education and supplemented the cognitive learning process with affective perspectives. The term *affective*, which specifically refers to the emotional dimensions of teaching, has popularly been expanded to include attitudes, values, morals, and spiritual aspects of living in addition to emotions. In dealing with these sometimes sensitive and personal issues in the classroom, teachers must make the discussion nonbiased and personalized without the influence of peers. Various types of affective imagery help to make the productive treatment of the affective dimension of topics possible, because the strategy allows the student to tune out external influences and focus on his/her feelings and experiences. Affective imagery can be further classified as *emotional imagery, spiritual imagery*, and *values clarification imagery*. The most important function of all types of affective imagery is to facilitate in the decision-making process.

Emotions can be treated in basically three ways using emotional imagery. Attempting to gain empathy for the health dilemmas of special groups is a function of emotional imagery. The students would, in their minds, become a member of that special group and feel the emotions of the dilemma. For example, students could experience a scenario that would mentally have them become disabled, poor, aged, or diseased. Another empathetical function would be to reverse roles with a significant other such as a parent or sweetheart so as to help with understanding and communication. As a component of the decision-making process, emotional imagery focuses mentally on the emotional aspects of a decision that is made before the actual decision is made. Feeling the emotions of the projected behavior helps to clarify the decision. Another function of emotional imagery is to deal with the emotion itself rather than in association with a topic. For example, having the student feel and deal with anger or love as an emotion is appropriate when studying the emotion.

Perhaps the most difficult aspect of the affective domain to include in the public classroom is the spiritual dimension or component of topics. The term *spiritual* generally represents a "red flag," and an immediate response is that "we cannot include the spiritual components in the classroom because of the "separation of church and state." If spiritual is defined as basic morals, integrity, sense of good and bad, of fulfillment, relying on a more powerful source for strength, or congruence of mind and body, then the spiritual may be dealt with. In many cases, it encompasses the concepts in religion, which is also a part of the spiritual dimension. Formerly, it was difficult to deal with in the class, but now, by merely allowing the students time to get in tune individually with their spiritual selves, whether that be a communication with diety, communing with nature, meditating, or practicing religious rituals mentally, the students can be allowed to do those things because they are doing it individually. The spiritual dimension is important because most decisions that are made must consider the individual's basic moral philosophy.

Similar to the popular values clarification strategies, values clarification imagery can perform similar functions such as values voting, critical incidents, moral dilemmas, values ranking, and other values clarification methods. The difference in doing values clarification in an imagery method is that instead of discussing the issues with the class and sometimes being encouraged to make public stands on issues (although this is not done as often as a few years ago) or voting, with others being able to witness the student's vote, the students isolate themselves, put themselves mentally into the valuing situation, and then resolve the issue privately without the influence of peers. Performing values clarification imagery enhances the power of the values clarification method.

DECISION-MAKING IMAGERY

Decision-making imagery focuses on the steps of the decision-making process. The first two steps of the decision-making process are information gathering and clarifying values, which have been mentioned as affective and cognitive imagery. Exploring the consequences of alternative solutions to the problem or decision (consequence imagery) and preparing for the implementation of the decision (simulation imagery) are major functions of decision-making imagery.

With every behavioral concept in education there are alternative choices for the student. The options at least include doing the particular behavior or not doing the behavior. Of course for most issues there are varied degrees of performing behaviors, such as the extent of fitness training, the degree of nutritional choices, or amount of stress management practices. Through consequence imagery, the outcomes or consequences of each of the behaviors can be explored to facilitate the decision-making process. The instructor can encourage students to select viable options or alternatives and, through consequence imagery, follow the life-style patterns that the option would direct. Depending on the nature of the behavior, the life-style exploration may be for immediate results or necessitate projection into the years ahead. For example, in relation to the decision of engaging in physical intimacy with someone before marriage, the feeling after the experience or abstinence should be considered perhaps the morning after and again several years into the future, considering that perhaps the couple remains together, and, again, if the couple did not stay together.

Just as the concept of simulation games has emerged as a means of approximating actual situations for group activities, so the concept of simulation imagery can approximate a behavioral situation in the mind. In an applied sense, once a decision has been made, based on information and clarified values, and all the viable alternatives have been explored, then rehearsal of how, when, and in what conditions the implementation of the behavior will occur can be imagined. The scene that will be imagined will be the scene(s) that best provides an opportunity for the decision to be enacted or the behavior implemented. It may be that the scene will be to avoid a behavior or say no to offers to enact a behavior such as drinking, taking drugs, or getting into the car of a drunk driver.

LIFE-STYLING IMAGERY

Life-styling is a popular term used in Health Education, which focuses on behavior changes that improve the health status of the individual. *Life-styling imagery* focuses on the behaviors that should be incorporated into the life-style. It is assumed that the decision process has been complete, and it becomes the task of the individual actually to modify his/her life. Life-styling uses the method of life-styling imagery in three major functions, including *role assumption imagery, habit breaking/forming imagery,* and *recreational imagery.*

Role assumption imagery is a method that allows the student to create an ideal image of what he/she would like to become. The generalized role becomes specific when topics are discussed and the students create the image relative to the topic area. The students rehearse the ideal image, attempting to convince themselves that they can develop the characteristics in the ideal. The principle is analogous to the rabbit that leads the dogs in a dog race, that is keeping the goal in sight for clear direction. The goals may focus on the social, spiritual, physical, emotional, or intellectual domains or even more specifically in areas such as marijuana use, stress management skills, etc.

Basic to psychotherapy is the process of helping people to overcome phobias, break habits, and eliminate undesirable behaviors by mentally associating a noxious image with the negative behavior. In classrooms where behaviors are encouraged or discouraged, habit breaking imagery can be accomplished by a class in a universal experience of breaking the same habit, if they all have the same habit, such as a class of smokers trying to quit smoking.

At other times it is better to have the students individually identify a behavior they want to change and have a universal noxious element to associate with the individual behavior. In the positive sense, habits that are desirable generally can be applicable to a diverse class. Socially accepted habits such as courtesy, assertiveness, and fitness development can generally be improved by associating the habit with a positive image. Habit forming imagery and habit breaking imagery are usually initiated in class and then encouraged to be carried with the students outside of class where the behavioral opportunity exists.

Recreational imagery is a function of imagery that encourages students to enjoy an imaginary situation. It is an escape from reality for a few moments. A basic approach to stress management is to relax when stressful moments are pressing, letting the student's mind go to a favorite recreational, restful place. Physiologically and psychologically this gives the mind and body a brief rest and acts as a refresher to continue to face the stressors again. Recreational imagery is used also in drug education to depict drug trips or substituted for drugs to help students escape reality, but in this case it is controlled.

Psychomotor imagery is a type of simulation imagery that functions in a life-styling mode. For years instructors in physical education and athletics have endorsed the idea of mental practice in perfecting physical skills. The mental rehearsal idea is also functional for other courses with psychomotor skill refinement as a component. Instruction in cardiopulmonary resuscitation, bandaging, airway obstruction, woodwork, ceramics, art, and music are all conducive to psychomotor imagery.

EDUCATIONAL IMAGERY MODEL

Courses at the university, secondary, and elementary levels vary as to cognitive, affective, and behavioral outcomes of the course. Many courses focus mainly on the cognitive objectives, such as some chemistry, biology, English grammar, and mathematics courses. Other courses such as health education, social studies, psychology, safety education, and physical education encourage students to make wise decisions and incorporate desired behaviors into their life-styles. Decisions related to drug use, human sexuality, driver safety, physical fitness, social health, and overcoming prejudices and stereotypes tend to expand the concept of education to facilitate decision making and improving the students' life-styles.

Depending on the focus of the course, whether it includes only the cognitive, includes the cognitive and the affective, or includes the cognitive, affective, behavioral, and decision-making functions, educational imagery functions to facilitate the process as has been described earlier. Figure 1-1 demonstrates the flow of functions as they branch from the cognitive to include the affective, decision-making, and life-styling (behavioral) dimensions. The left side of the model describes what type of course is appropriate for the type of imagery that is described in that area. The model may be applicable only for cognitive imagery for those who only use cognitive strategies. The expansion to the affective has become popular in recent years and is the next step. Taking time to deal with decisions and allowing students to make decisions about their personal lives is the next step and is facilitated by simulation imagery. Psychomotor and life-styling imagery follows and is particularly useful for teachers who include behavioral foci in their teaching. The model provides a framework to exemplify the functions and hopefully triggers some thought in the reader as to the applicability of the strategy in his or her own teaching environment.

CONFLUENT NATURE OF EDUCATIONAL IMAGERY

Educational imagery exemplifies the concept of confluent education, that is the blending of cognitive, affective, and behavioral dimensions of education. Educational imagery strategies can be developed that will focus on one function or include all the functions. A simulation imagery strategy could be used to develop a scene that provided the student with a challenging decision to lend help or seek help with a victim of a cardiac arrest. It also becomes an emotional strategy in the sense that the anxiety, fear, and caring feelings would be emphasized at the tragic scene. It is also a psychomotor strategy because the trained student will likely practice the skill of cardiopulmonary resuscitation by mentally rehearsing the sequence of checking for consciousness, tilting the head, checking for respiration, etc. The rhythm of compressions

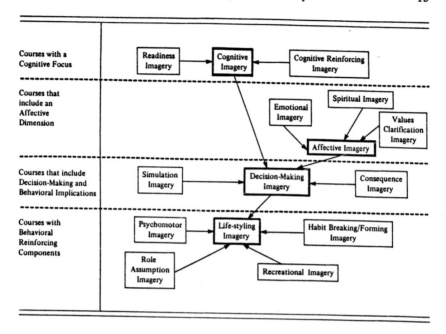

Figure 1-1. Educational imagery in the educational process.

to breathe, depth of the compression, positioning of hands, etc. would be rehearsed. It seems that there are an unlimited number of confluent combinations that could be developed for different content areas and issues.

The next chapter provides an overview of the contributions to and origins of educational imagery.

Chapter 2

THE ROOTS OF
EDUCATIONAL IMAGERY

"Guided Imagery," "Directed Fantasies," "Outcome Psycho-drama," "Mental Practice," "Visualization," "Systematic Desensitization," "Mind Play," "Brain Games," "Meditation," "Forced Fantasies," and "Mind Games" are but a few of the names that have been applied to the idea of using one's own imagination to promote one's mental, physical, social, emotional, and spiritual well-being. The purpose of this chapter is not to give an in-depth analysis of the use of imagery in psychotherapy or physical education but only to share with the reader some of the functional uses of imagery in helping individuals. It would be a long, involved chapter to cite all the therapists and scientists who have used imagery in some form, because it is a basic tool in the process of psychotherapy. For the reader who is interested in a more detailed account of the use of imagery in psychotherapy, either *Psychotherapy Through Imagery* by Shorr (1974) or *Imagery and Daydream in Psychotherapy and Behavior Modification* by Singer (1974) is recommended. The concept of educational imagery is built upon the foundation of the basic principles of imagery in psychotherapy and physical education and from these roots acquires its credibility.

Even though men and women have always been fascinated by their imaginations, it was not until the eighteenth century, when Muratori wrote a treatise called *On the Power of Human Imagination,* that the study of the imagination began (Singer, 1974). It was not until the twentieth century that imagery began to be redefined and became a valuable tool in psychotherpy. Freud's "concentration technique" in 1892 helped him sense the nature of individuals as he would press on their foreheads and the patients would share the images they would see. Freud, through psychoanalysis, would interpret those images. Even though Freud eventually gave up the free imagery method, it is felt that if he would have continued with it psychotherapy would have been more advanced today (Singer, 1974).

Carl Jung, in 1913, developed the concept of "active imagination," which resulted from his own self-analysis as he let his imagination roam and attempted to bring his own subconscious out through dreams and imagination. Each image that he encountered during his imagery he analyzed. According to Ellenberger (1970), Jung found himself digging underground caves and galleries and encountered many strange figures. He began later to use the same strategy with his patients.

Phenomenology, the study of how people see the world, explores the use of the imagination to ready people to perceive, anticipate, defend, and act upon events to come. The varying images often become sources of conflict because when two people prepare or anticipate a situation separately, they enter the situation with two different images of what is to transpire. Thus, when "he thinks of her in one light, she thinks of him in another," and the conflict follows (Laing, 1962).

More recently, in 1955, Fromm encouraged the therapist to move away from the conventional free association procedure, that is analyzing whatever jumped into the patients mind, and suggested that therapists use their creativity and design scenarios for their patients and analyze reactions to the scenarios. Desoille (1965), who was an engineer, developed the "Guided Affective Imagery" (GAI) and is credited with being the reference point for nearly all psychotherapeutic developments evolving later that employed imagery as the primary approach method. In the GAI the patient is initiated into a relaxed state using a procedure approximating Jacobsen's "progressive relaxation" method and then encouraged to imagine specific images such as a seashore, then relocate him/herself in the environment. The client was then guided through specific activities within the selected environment depending on the nature of the psychological problem.

Wolpe's (1969) "systematic desensitization" relies heavily upon clear images to be effective in helping the patient overcome
phobias and other problems. The patients begin with images that
are moderately anxiety producing and progress eventually to images that produce high anxiety; when they are able to cope with
the clear images, then they are more likely to be able to cope with
the situation in reality. Using the same approach, "implosive therapy," developed by Stampfl (1967), encourages the patients to
imagine the worst possible outcomes of a particular fear or ob-
session that they are having, and as they reinact the outcome in
their minds, they become desensitized; then, in reality, the disas-
trous images rarely come about. Maddi (1970) states that the function of imagination in preparation for action is so potent and
natural that even the fear of the consequences of the action cannot inhibit mental preparation entirely.

There are major efforts to have people develop their imagery
skills. Gold (1980) cites scenarios designed to practice and improve imagery skills that lead people into vast gardens, visualizing
orange trees, picking up the oranges, feeling them, tasting them,
and enjoying them. Whole books have been dedicated solely to
the development of imagery skills without the major functions included in educational imagery.

A component of Maultsby's Rational Self Counseling is the
practice of Rational Emotive Imagery, which allows clients to
practice, through imagery, the emotional and behavior responses
that are consistent with previously developed rational thought and
rational self-analysis (Maultsby, 1978). The two types of imagery
are therapeutic imagery (overcoming fears and phobias and also
facilitating growth into areas of behavior that the patient has not
yet attempted) and auto-adversive imagery (overcoming compul-
sive behaviors by pairing the behaviors with exceptionally noxious
images) (Maultsby, 1971).

As a component of the decision-making process when counseling individuals, Janis and Mann (1977) describe the process of
"outcome psychodrama," which, in the counseling sense, allows
the client, through imagery, to visualize the outcomes of each of
the choices. For example, in counseling clients with marital problems, the clients are instructed to imagine their lives one year into

the future twice, once having divorced their spouses and the second time remaining together. Their results were very positive in bringing out new information and facilitating decisions.

Perhaps Singer (1974, 1980) and Lazarus (1977) have done more to focus on the concept of imagery as a tool and a benefit for well people than anyone in recent times. In Singer's book *Mind Play*, a popular lay book, yet based on numerous studies including many of his own, Singer describes that fantasy and daydreams may be the most human quality and evolution's greatest gift to mankind. Fantasies and daydreams allow humans to master the environment in ways that no other living being can, reports Singer. "We can entertain ourselves, educate ourselves, and enrich our lives in a number of ways without the use of any materials except our minds" (Singer, 1980). He also represents the use of imagery as a powerful constructive force for living, self-fulfillment, and guiding our future in constructive ways. Singer rejects the unfortunate negative connotation the term "daydreaming" has gained, symbolizing wasting time and energy when in fact it can be a productive force. Singer provides guidelines where imagery and daydreams can be used to reduce stress, plan for a more effective future, gain control over undesirable habits, become more sensitive to moods and needs of others, increase sexual pleasure, enhance creativity in daily living as well as in artistic and scientific expression, learn more about oneself, amuse oneself in idle moments, avoid boredom, deal with loneliness of old age, and even make it possible to confront one's own death with dignity.

Another respected psychotherapist, Arnold Lazarus, in his book *In the Mind's Eye* (1977), describes very practical approaches to building confidence and skill, overcoming fears and anxieties, dealing with children's fears, overcoming bad habits, dealing with sadness and despondency, overcoming psychosomatic disorders, and preventing and preparing for future problems through imagery. He also cites the importance of imagery by giving the example of two people who had a car wreck and each sustained permanent disabling injuries. One was suicidal and depressed; the other, optimistic. The difference in the two was imagery: one's images focused on what he had lost and was despondent; the other focused on what he still had and was optimistic.

Another root of educational imagery is in the currently popular area of stress management. A basic approach to stress management is in the form of relaxation training. During relaxation training, individuals first find comfortable positions and sometimes tense the muscle groups in their bodies progressively and then relax them to note the difference in the tensed and relaxed state (approximating Jacobsen's progressive relaxation, 1974). This procedure is generally accompanied by deep breathing and focusing on various muscle groups in the body. The imagery component of relaxation comes into play by imagining the air going in and out of the lungs. In Yoga, often the focus will be on an external part of the being. Sometimes the person relaxing will imagine becoming very light or very heavy and a wide variety of other imagining exercises. Perhaps the most enjoyable and effective for school situations, in the experience of the author, is the trip to a favorite place. The students are instructed to go to a place that is out of doors, real or imaginary, where they can imagine themselves lying down, feeling the perfect temperature, hearing sounds, such as birds singing, rushing water, or breezes in the trees. They can see grass, water, or whatever they elect to have at their favorite place as long as it is relaxing. It is the stress management technique that triggered much of the concept of educational imagery.

Imagery or "mental practice" has proven by many studies to be an effective tool in improving psychomotor performance in a wide variety of sports and games. Skaters, skiers, basketball players, football players, gymnasts, jumpers, dancers, raquetball players, and many other competitors can improve their skills through imagery. Alan Richardson in 1967 reported on some thirty studies of mental practice, and he concluded, "despite a variety of methodological inadequacies, the trend of most studies indicates that mental practice procedures are associated with improved performances on the task."

There is beginning to be increasing evidence to support the efficacy of mental practice on a physiological level. Some researchers are noting by studying electroencephalograms that neuronal impulses fired across the cortex of the brain during an actual performance of a skill are also fired during the mental practice of the same skill. Davidson and Schwartz report "predictable shifts in

EEG asymetry have been found to accompany both overt behavioral tasks as well as covert tasks requiring the self generation of imagery in specific cognitive modes" (1977). The implications of this information are tremendous to the validity of the use of imagery in the classroom. This book is intended to trigger the reader's thinking relevant to these potential uses.

The next chapter deals with educational imagery preparation in the classroom atmosphere for the instructor and the students.

Chapter 3

IMPLEMENTATION OF EDUCATIONAL IMAGERY IN THE CLASSROOM

E ducational imagery, because it is a new teaching strategy for the classroom, must be implemented with some caution until the method of teaching becomes more common. Sometimes, from the perspective of an uninformed observer, the educational imagery strategy appears to be something strange and nonproductive when, in fact, it has the power to be a potential motivating and facilitating educational force.

This chapter will describe several recommendations for the following stages of strategy implementation:

1. Classroom atmosphere and teacher preparation
2. Introduction and preparation of the student
3. Presenting the educational imagery strategy
4. Closure and processing educational imagery.

CLASSROOM ATMOSPHERE AND TEACHER PREPARATION

Before considering using educational imagery, it is important for the teacher to recognize educational objectives that can be accomplished through the use of imagery. The problem with innovative teaching methods such as values clarification, simulation games, and now educational imagery is that they can be fun to do and interesting, and sometimes teachers use them in the classroom as time fillers, to make the class fun, without really accomplishing an educational objective. If the purpose of the strategy is to help students make decisions regarding behavior, to reinforce cognitive information, explore the affective dimension of being, or any other productive function of educational imagery, and an educational or behavioral objective can be written for using the method, then the teacher should proceed.

Depending on the nature and function of educational imagery, the teacher must make a decision whether to be directive or nondirective. For cognitive strategies and psychomotor strategies where there is a correct and incorrect answer or procedure, then the teacher can be directive, that is, lead the student through the scenario without allowing for individual decisions. Where educational imagery is most effective is with decision-making and affective strategies that allow the students to put individual interpretations and decisions into the scenario. In these cases, the teacher should be nondirective. Nondirective indicates that the teacher will lead the students into the scenario but at appropriate points allow the students to complete the picture based on their own information, values, and other factors. What is important is that all scenarios, whether directive or nondirective, are described in such a fashion that all students can experience the strategy.

The classroom atmosphere by design is usually detrimental to educational imagery. The lights are bright to be less stressful on the students' eyes when reading, the floors are hard for easy cleaning and longer wear, and the desks are straight back to support the students in a studious position. To imagine the scenarios that the teacher will present to the students, the students will need to concentrate very hard with limited distractions. They should become unaware of other students, be comfortable, relaxed, and be in the mood of the scenario. One classroom arrangement that can aid to attain the students' optimal state to do imagery is to dim the lights so that students will not be distracted visually. If there are windows in the classroom, then the room can be darkened as when showing films or slides by drawing the opaque curtains. Additionally, the students can sit comfortably in their chairs with a straight back and their head and neck muscles relaxed. The more daring teacher might have students lying down on the floor for comfort. There are some obvious precautions with dimming the lights and putting children on the floor to do educational imagery. Precautions regarding this are cited in Chapter 11. Ideally there would be blankets or mats on the floor for student comfort.

Selected props in the classroom introducing or during the strategy might be appropriate. For example, if the students were going to make decisions at a party, then some background party music would help their imaginations. If a hospital room is to be imagined, then some smells of rubbing alcohol would be helpful. If the student is to imagine being out-of-doors, then a fan for gentle breezes, tree scented room fresheners, or a recording of birds, and rushing creeks would add effect. It should be noted that in the examples cited to this point there were no visual props, because during the actual strategy the students will have their eyes closed. For introducing the strategy, the teacher could have some props that would help the students to imagine when their eyes were closed. For example, alcohol bottles, marijuana joints, or hard drugs could be displayed and discussed prior to a drug imagery strategy, or human anatomy models could be displayed when doing strategies related to the cognitive reinforcing of body functions.

The last element of the classroom arrangement that should be mentioned is that of space. The students' desks or chairs, if moveable, should be such that students are not close enough to touch each other. Where overcrowding is a problem and students do not have enough space to keep from touching each other and if desks are immovable, then the teacher may want to go outside in good weather or not do the strategy at all. The atmosphere must be right for the strategy, but in most classrooms with minor modifications as mentioned, the atmosphere is such that it can provide students with a rich, unique experience.

One other point of preparation should be noted before doing educational imagery. For the person who is experienced and has used educational imagery, then there is little question of the value. However, if a casual observer, administrator, or parent were to witness a classroom of students closing their eyes in a darkened room and the teacher leading the students into a decision-making scenario, it could give the observer reason to question the teacher's methods. It is advised then to inform superiors or parents of the method to avoid potential misunderstandings.

INTRODUCTION AND PREPARATION OF THE STUDENT

The first time teachers use educational imagery, they may want to introduce the students to the strategy by saying something similar to the following (assuming the students are going to be making choices during the strategy):

> We are going to do something a little different today to apply the concepts we have learned about (*topic*). I'd like you to imagine in your minds as clearly as you can the scenes I will describe to you. There will be a time where I will have you complete the scene, or story, and I will allow plenty of time for that. I'd like you to see in your mind's eye the things around you. Imagine the sounds you would hear, the smells you would smell, and perhaps the feel of the things you touch. If there are emotions that would arise from the situation, let yourself feel those emotions.

In reference to the students focusing on the sensations, there has been information published in journals indicating the ease as well as the difficulty that some people have trying to imagine different sensations in the scenario. The more the students can imagine, the more effective the imagery strategy. Depending on the nature of the scenario, the following senses may be practiced to improve imagery skills.

SENSE	DESCRIPTION	HOW TO PRACTICE
Visual	Seeing the scenes with shape and color	Visualize the colors in the rainbow or look at an object and then close your eyes and see it in your mind's eye.
Auditory	Hearing the sounds in the scene	Imagine the sound of a train whistle, thunder, a glass breaking, the wind in the trees.
Cutaneous	Sensing how something feels to the touch	Imagine the touch of cotton, of a pin point, or of sandpaper.
Kinesthetic	Seeing action or movement	See someone walking up stairs, a child on a swing, someone dancing.
Gustatory	Sensing the taste of something	Taste the bite into a sweet, juicy orange, or taste the bite of a sour lemon.

SENSE	DESCRIPTION	HOW TO PRACTICE
Olfactory	Sensing the smell of something	Smell the smoke from a campfire or bread baking in the oven.
Physiological	Sensing the bodily state or feeling	Imagine being sleepy or the feeling of having an upset stomach.
Affective	Feeling the emotions of a situation	Imagine bubbling with happiness, totally in love, or very angry.

Another area that has been discussed in the literature is the difficulty of some people being able to project themselves into the scene. It seems easy for some to visualize a scenario as if they were there and looking around, but when it comes to seeing themselves in the scenario as an observer, then it becomes more difficult. This information is important when presenting and preparing a scenario so that the teacher will not lose students by having them project themselves into the scene when the strategy could be just as effective by not doing so. Scenarios can be presented and worded in such a way that the students can either imagine themselves in the scene or they can visualize the things around them as if they were in the scene.

If the teacher speculates that the students might not be able to complete the educational imagery strategy without giggling or having some students causing distractions, the following challenge to the students following the introduction cited earlier has worked well in numerous occasions, particularly when working with adolescents:

> I want you to know that the strategy we are about to use has been used mostly with junior, senior, and graduate university students (which is true as far as the author knows). There was some question in the minds of some as to whether you have the maturity to handle this method. I think you do. We will try it, to see if you have the power to concentrate on what I say and ignore everyone else in the classroom. It is difficult but I think you can do it.

Generally students respond to the addendum by wanting to show the teacher how mature they can be, and problems of disruptions during the strategy rarely occur. To prepare the students further, the introduction would continue as follows:

> I want you to get as comfortable as you can (either in their chairs or on the floor) and close your eyes (to avoid visual distractions) and be quiet. I would like you to isolate yourselves from the rest of the class in your mind by consciously relaxing.

The word *relax* here is a key word. When the students get accustomed to doing educational imagery strategies, then the students will relax autogenously, that is will be trained to relax and will respond almost immediately by clearing their heads of extraneous thoughts and relaxing the muscles of their bodies. It is recommended that initially the students learn to relax systematically. The purpose of relaxing students is that relaxation training puts the students in a state of mind where they are isolated from the rest of the class mentally, and uncomfortable parts of the body will not be distractors to the educational imagery strategy. The class essentially "warms up" their concentration skills and becomes ready for the teacher's guidance. The active process of relaxation allows students to concentrate on breathing and muscle groups, which diverts attention from others in the class and helps the students to respond to the teacher's voice. There are numerous ways of doing relaxation training, but the following are suggested for no other reason than that they have been used effectively with children, adolescents, and university students by the author.

Deep breathing is a method of relaxation that serves to focus the thoughts of students on their inner selves and away from the environment. To have the students do the breathing, the instructor may say something like the following:

> I would like you to get into a comfortable position either sitting or laying down and try to relax. Take a deep, cleansing breath, let it out (pause), and then take another deep breath and hold it for five seconds (pause); let it out and feel the tenseness leave your body. As you continue to take deep breaths, concentrate on the relaxation and tension relief you feel each time you exhale. Concentrate only on your breathing.

Muscle relaxation is an exercise method for beginning students and can be administered in a variety of ways, but one that approximates Jacobson's progressive relaxation (1974) is appropriate. Consider the following monologue to promote muscle relaxation:

> I am going to have you focus on selected parts of your body. I want you to tense and then relax the muscles in that area. The reason is so that you can sense the difference between tensed and relaxed states of the muscles. First focus on your feet, and on my command I want you to flex the muscles in your feet by curling your toes on both feet. Ready, flex! (hold for five seconds) and relax, and feel the marked difference from the tense to the relaxed state; feel the tenseness drain from your feet. Your feet are now totally relaxed. Focus now on your lower leg muscles, and on my command I would like you to flex the calf muscle by pointing your toes and flexing the muscle. Okay, Flex! (hold for five seconds) Now relax and feel the tension leave your calf muscles; it feels so good and relaxed. Your feet and lower leg are so relaxed they almost feel as though they are floating.

This exercise continues, having the students focus on the rest of the general muscle groups of the body. The progression would include the upper leg muscles, the hand (making a fist), the forearm, the biceps, the abdominal muscles, the shoulder and neck muscles, and then the facial muscles. With children and adolescents, it is advisable to save time to have the students focus and flex several muscle groups such as the whole leg, including the foot, calf, and upper leg, the whole arm, the trunk, and neck, shoulder and facial muscles together. If too much time is spent on muscle relaxation, then there will be less time for the functions of imagery. The whole process can take as long as fifteen minutes, but for educational imagery, the process should be condensed to three to five minutes.

When the students have flexed all their muscles and then relaxed them, reassure them how relaxed they are, and sometimes you can tell them that they feel light as though they are floating, perhaps on a cloud. Another thing they can imagine is that they are in a rowboat with a mattress on the bottom of the boat and they are lying down rocking gently with the ripples of water. (Some people have an adversity to water and may not relax with the rowboat imagery.)

After the students have been guided into relaxation several times, they will eventually be able to get relaxed on their own, autogenously. The students, upon hearing the teacher's command "relax," will focus on different muscle groups, not tensing, since they are experienced at telling the difference between tension and relaxation, and relax each muscle group on their own in a matter of several seconds.

A third approach uses the last component of muscle relaxation training and that is to have the students clear their minds of worries and other extraneous thoughts by having them focus on something. One of the best approaches is to have them go to a favorite place in their minds where they can relax, concentrate on a favorite word, imagine doing something they like to do, or have them focus on the center of the body, perhaps the heart, and feel it pounding and tune into its rhythm.

PRESENTING THE EDUCATIONAL IMAGERY STRATEGY

When leading the students into an educational imagery scenario, the primary focus of the students must be on the images in their minds and not on the instructor's voice. The teacher then must soften his/her voice so that all can hear yet soft enough to be secondary in the students' minds. It is advised that a teacher use a tape recorder in private to practice voice levels, and if the teacher can make his or her own voice secondary, the students will be able to also.

The pauses of silence are critical in educational imagery. If the students are to make decisions, imagine scenes, clarify values, or perform other functions, they need to have time to imagine those things. Located within the strategies in the chapters that follow are the notations of appropriate places for pauses. The length of the pause will vary depending on the nature of the preceding instructions of the teacher. The best way to know the length of the pause is for the teacher actually to do the imagery at the same time as the students. It is important for the teacher to "get into" the strategy and imagine the images that the students are asked to visualize. When the instructor finishes the imagery task, and buffers that time with a few more seconds, it usually allows the students time to complete the imagery task.

Sometimes there is a fear of silence by teachers. Having the class totally silent seems a waste of time, and worries surface about students losing their concentration. Experience has shown that, most of the time, students are not given enough time to complete the active imagination process.

It is also recommended that the instructor not read the strategy, because there may be a lack of meaning and difficulty reading, particularly if the lights are dimmed. If the students sense the instructor is reading the strategy, it has a tendency to lose some of the effectiveness as opposed to the teacher who gets a feel for the strategy and then relates it in his or her own words. It is easier for the teacher to imagine the scenarios and share in the students experience and thereby process the strategy better. The teacher who is most effective using educational imagery is the teacher who merely describes the images that he/she sees while guiding the students, as long as biases are avoided.

CLOSURE AND PROCESSING EDUCATIONAL IMAGERY

Following the educational imagery strategy, with the lights on, the students in their chairs, and your speaking primary in their thinking, it is important to "check out" each student to be sure that everything is back to normal. In three years of using the educational imagery strategy with over 2,000 different students of different ages, there has never been any kind of problem. The only potential problem that could arise might be if the student were bordering on a mental breakdown, and with clear images, a negative reaction could possibly be triggered. The likelihood of this happening is very rare, especially if the images are positive and are geared toward making the student feel good.

For small groups, the best way of checking the status of the students following an imagery strategy is merely to ask them questions such as

Was this a bad experience for anyone?

Was this a helpful experience; were you able to see the applicability?

How well were you able to envision the scenarios?

When faced with a condition similar to the one you imagined, do you think you will respond the same as you did in your imagination?

Did anyone not like the strategy?

For larger classes, the students can break up into dyads or larger groups and discuss the outcomes of the strategy, assuring that everyone has had a healthy experience. It is not that students should not be sad or concerned if they have learned something about themselves that they did not know and may want to change, for that is the purpose. However, to be severely upset by the experience is what should be avoided. The way to check to see is by asking the questions. The answers are not that important, but getting everyone talking is.

During the process of assuring the positive nature of the experience, the teacher needs to come to closure on the method. The question " So what?" should be asked by the students. That is to say, how is it that I am benefitting by imagining this scenario? Were values clarified? If so, why is it important to have them clarified? Will it help me to make behaviorial decisions? Did the strategy better prepare me to deal with future issues such as career choices, peer influenced drug choices, interpersonal relationships, etc.? Did the strategy reinforce a cognitive concept? To justify the use of imagery there must be an educational objective that must be fulfilled. Then, when processing and discussing the strategy, the objective must be brought out and explained in clear terms to the students.

The next chapter will introduce imagery strategies that are geared toward cognitive concepts. In addition to the major concept of cognitive imagery, two major functions of cognitive imagery including readiness imagery and cognitive reinforcing imagery will be discussed.

Chapter 4

COGNITIVE IMAGERY

DECISION MAKING

- **Giving Information about the Decision — Cognitive Imagery**
- Clarifying Values, Attitudes, and Emotions
- Looking at Alternative Solutions or Options
- Exploring the Consequences to the Alternatives
- Making and Planning to Implement the Decision
- Implementing and Adhering to the Decision

There has been much written on the nature of learning, but definitions, approaches, and theories of learning vary. To explore the vast number of learning theories is not within the scope of this book, but an endorsement for the method of educational imagery lies in the cognitivist's perspective of the nature of learning. The cognitivist perceives that basic human nature is dynamic and each individual is unique with an ability to perceive, remember, think, and control his/her actions. On the other hand, the behaviorists view the human beginning as a blank slate to be written upon, with environmental experiences producing the writing upon the slate which, over time, results in the human becoming a product of his/her experiences. The nature of educational imagery is such that it supplements the behaviorist's concepts of feeding the human system but endorses the cognitivist's perspective by allowing time for the students to process, interpret, and personalize the concepts through their own abilities.

30

Educational psychologists have noted for years that the function of imagery in human memory is to improve the level of retention when comparing memory associated with only verbal meanings. Richardson (1980) has noted that imagery is an important facilitating tool for long- and short-term memory. Studies have shown that to take seemingly unrelated words such as *cat* and *tricycle* and encourage students to remember that association will result, over time, in a 46 percent recall of that association. If an image of the association is formed, such as the cat riding the tricycle, the retention approaches 71 percent (DuBois et al., 1979). Sommer (1978) concurs that learning is faster in high sensory content and that those areas which are high in imagery or develop clear images are recalled better than those areas which are not.

Cognitive imagery, using the concept of incorporating images into the learning and memorizing process, enhances long- and short-term memory. The teacher should use cognitive imagery to create images in the minds of students to facilitate the learning of dates and vocabulary, memorizing symbols, grasping concepts, etc. For example, the teacher who encourages the students to visualize a picture or symbol to associate vocabulary words to meanings will have more success than the teacher who has students memorize the verbal meanings only. If the English literature teacher desires the students to remember characters in a novel or short story, then the students should take time to visualize the characters during reading and when pondering after the reading. In chemistry, the visualization of two hydrogens attached to an oxygen to form a water molecule can facilitate the learning of molecular structure. Any imagery strategy that facilitates the learning process falls into the general category of cognitive imagery. Educational Imagery Strategy 1 is an example of a general cognitive imagery strategy. The strategies reported in this book will include the purpose of the strategy, the type of strategy as it relates to functions described in Chapter 1, and some examples of discussion questions and variations to the strategy. It is assumed that the preparation of the classroom and the students has occurred prior to the strategy as described in Chapter 3. The students are relaxed, mentally isolated, and have been prepared to visualize the scenarios (*see* Education Imagery Strategy 1, Appendix).

Although there are many ways in which cognitive imagery can aid in the learning process, two specific functions will be described in this chapter. The first function is to help students prepare for the information they are about to receive and is called *readiness imagery*. The second function is to repeat or reinforce the information or concept to commit it to memory, and this is called *cognitive reinforcing imagery*.

READINESS IMAGERY

For teaching to be most effective, students need to be ready to receive the information that is to be presented by the teacher. Additionally, the students should be able to see the relevance of the information they will receive. Both of these functions can be accomplished through readiness imagery. To accomplish the functions, the teacher, prior to presenting, prepares the class with images or pictures in the mind that (1) generate curiosity about the subject, (2) describe the circumstances or conditions related to the subject (such as the discovery of the principle or invention, or the writing of the piece of literature), (3) set the mood or create an atmosphere for the events to follow and (4) describe a problem or dilemma that can be solved or prevented by the information that follows the readiness imagery strategy.

Specifically, in English literature, the reading of a novel such as *A Tale of Two Cities* by Dickens could be introduced by having the students mentally picture a scenario that describes the political, social, religious, and health concerns of the era described in *A Tale of Two Cities*. The innovative English teacher can have the students go back in time, perhaps in a time machine, and spend a day living as a child might have lived in that century to appreciate and prepare for the reading of the novel.

The same concept can be used in history, where students could spend some time mentally exploring the thoughts of Benjamin Franklin, George Washington, John Adams, or perhaps the thoughts and life-style of a typical colonist near the time of the signing of the Declaration of Independence. How much more meaningful could the singing of the "Star Spangled Banner" be if a music teacher could paint in the minds of the students the scenario that Francis Scott Key might have seen when he awoke aboard ship to see the Stars and Stripes waving after a night of cannon bombardment.

The physics teacher could paint a picture of a hot air balloon and a person inside could drop a marble out of the balloon. The students could imagine the flight of the marble as it accelerated toward the earth and try to visualize how fast the marble might be traveling, attempting to grasp the concept of gravity, acceleration, and falling bodies. As they questioned the speed and perhaps the damage it could do, they would ready themselves for the appropriate formulas. Likewise, the chemistry teacher might describe scenarios of people getting acid burns and alkaline burns prior to a discussion of laboratory safety. Educational Imagery Strategies 2 and 3 typify readiness imagery strategies. (*see* Appendix)

COGNITIVE REINFORCING IMAGERY

It is well known that memory relies on repetition to be assured that the brain will store the information either in short- or long-term memory stores. Most often in education, the teacher gives the information once and perhaps during a review for a test, but the real memorization is left to the student. The problem is that it seems redundant for the teacher to repeat the same thing that he/she had just presented solely for the sake of repetition. Cognitive reinforcing imagery strategies provide an interesting, unique, and reinforcing approach to encouraging students to retain the desired information and concepts. Educational Imagery Strategies 4 and 5 are examples of cognitive reinforcing imagery that reinforce the understanding of the anatomy and physiology of the human circulatory system and the life cycle of the king salmon fish. The "Fantastic Voyage" is obviously a take off on the movie by the same title (*see* Educational Imagery Strategies 4 and 5, Appendix).

The next chapter will focus on affective imagery, which becomes an important step in the decision-making process, which will also be described in the next chapter. Although not mentioned to this point, the cognitive is very important in decision making, so actually cognitive imagery is also a step in the decision-making process, although the focus has been on the cognitive as a component of traditional education rather than a step in the decision-making process.

Appendix

EDUCATIONAL IMAGERY STRATEGIES

Educational Imagery Strategy 1

SIDE-ANGLE-SIDE

Purpose: To help students to remember that one way of proving two triangles congruent is to have two sides joined by an equal angle on both triangles.

Type: Directive; cognitive imagery

Monologue: Imagine in your minds any angle less than 180°. (pause) Attach to that angle a side with any length that you want to imagine. (pause) On the other side of the angle, imagine another side with any length that you can imagine. (pause) In your mind you should now see an angle with two sides of lengths that you have imagined. Try to imagine a way to connect the third leg to form a triangle and not have it be exactly the same size and shape of triangle every time you join ends of the angle.

Discussion:

1. Was there anyone who could complete the triangle two different ways?
2. Can you see how, given an angle and two sides of an angle, it proves that two triangles are in fact congruent?

Variations: Use other theorems, word problems, and other mathematical problems.

Educational Imagery Strategy 2
SNAKEBITE

Purpose: To stimulate students' curiosity and prepare them for a lesson on first aid for snakebites.

Type: Nondirective; cognitive readiness

Monologue: Visualize in your mind a friend with whom you would like to go hiking or walking. (pause) Picture him or her as clearly as you can in hiking or walking attire. (pause) Imagine now that you are walking along in a beautiful environment; visualize the surroundings; perhaps there are trees, (pause) water, (pause) grass. (pause) Listen to the sounds of the birds (pause) and rushing waters. (pause) Smell the smells associated with this beautiful environment. (pause) See your friend walking in front of you. Suddenly you hear a rattling noise. (pause) Along the side of the place that you are walking, you see a coiled rattlesnake, and before you can yell a warning, the snake strikes the leg of your friend; imagine this. (pause) Visualize the reaction that your friend would have. (pause) The snake has let go but is still nearby. Complete the scenario, deciding what you will do with the snake and how you would help your friend. (long pause)

Discussion:

1. How many of you were comfortable in helping your friend in this situation?
2. It is likely that some of you were far away from help and others were close. Knowing this, what were some of the things you did to help your friend?
3. What did you do with the snake?
4. Were you able to keep your "cool" and not panic in this situation?
5. Do you feel as though some instruction would help you to deal with this situation?

Variations: Any number of first aid situations could be used: drowning, bleeding, cardiac arrests, shock, fractured bones, poisoning, etc.

Educational Imagery Strategy 3
WOODSHOP SAFETY

Purpose: To prepare students to be receptive to information regarding shop safety.

Type: Directive; readiness

Monologue: I would like you to imagine that we are several weeks into the semester and are working on individual projects. Imagine the shop with classmates working. (pause) See all the tools, smell the wood, and sawdust. (pause) Visualize the type of article that you would like to make, look at the detail. (pause) Assume that you have completed the project except for one piece; imagine the project with one piece of wood lacking. (pause) Feel that you are excited to finish the project. (pause) Imagine taking the last piece of wood to fit into place and that there is just a little notch on the wood that needs to be removed and the project will be complete. Imagine walking quickly over to the table saw and switching it on. Imagine the sound of the table saw. (pause) Look at the details of the saw, the moving blade, the jigs and guide. (pause) Imagine putting the guides to the side and merely hand guiding the piece of wood to the saw. (pause) Imagine that the blade hits the wood at a wrong angle and the wood twists in your hand and throws your hand into the blade. (pause) The little notch of wood flies off and hits you in the eye, since you had no safety glasses on. If you wear glasses, imagine them shattering. (pause) Imagine how bad the wound on your hand would be, the pain, the embarrassment. (pause) Imagine the eye pain. (pause) Return your focus to now; you are not hurt, but only beginning.

Discussion:
1. How serious were the wounds that you inflicted upon yourself?
2. How could the hand wound have been prevented?
3. How could the eye wound have been prevented?

Precaution: If students are already apprehensive of using the power tools, then the strategy should be modified to paint a picture of someone doing things in a safe manner. Being overly cautious can be potentially as dangerous as not using good safety procedures.

Variations: Drill press, band saw, hand tools, etc. could be substituted for the table saw. Shop cleanliness could be emphasized by imagining tripping over clutter, etc.

Educational Imagery Strategy 4

FANTASTIC VOYAGE
(Circulatory System)

Purpose: To reinforce the information about the pathway and the function of the circulatory system.

Type: Directive; cognitive reinforcing

Monologue: We are going to take a ride through the circulatory system. To do this we are going to make you very small and put you into a clear plastic bubble and inject you into a vein of a man. Now imagine the clear plastic bubble with a clear chair inside; imagine opening the door and sitting down and strapping yourself in. (pause) The bubble is in a room with white walls and lots of laboratory instruments. (pause) You can see several doctors with white lab coats standing around you. (pause) From inside the bubble you can see that they have a shrinking gun that they point at you, and as it goes off visualize yourself and the bubble shrinking to the size of a blood cell. (pause) The doctors put you into a syringe and inject you into the vein of a man. It feels like a roller coaster as you rush down the needle and find yourself in the blood stream. (pause) Visualize the purplish blood cells that have been stripped of their oxygen molecules and now have carbon dioxide molecules on the sides. (pause) You can see the platelets and white blood cells (pictures should have been seen earlier so students can visualize them). (pause) You see the vein walls — they are "off white" and streaked with occasional placques. (pause) Your journey is very smooth as you travel up the inside of the arm, which is where you entered the vein. You notice that the tunnel you are in, the vein, is getting larger as you gently travel in your plastic bubble. (pause) You begin to hear now a noise going "lub dub," and you recognize that you are nearing the heart. The noise gets louder and louder until you see ahead the right atrium of the heart and know then that you are in the superior vena cava. (pause) As you float into the large atrium, you hear the loud slamming of the tricuspid valves. (pause) You can see the atrium contract and the triscuspid valves open up, and you rush into the ventricle. (pause) The cavity seems huge, but you are not there very long because the ventricle contracts and the loud rush of blood around you sends you through the pulmonary valve. Your movements are no longer smooth since you left the heart but in spurts. It feels as though you are taking off in a plane then stopping suddenly and starting again. (pause) You notice that the pulmonary arteries are getting smaller and that they are branching out. (pause) Eventually you fall in line with the purplish red blood cells with carbon dioxide molecules on them. The walls are just large enough for your plastic bubble to go through. You hear in the short distance the rushing of wind, and you know you are nearing the lungs. (pause) Then you witness the miracle exchange — you see that the walls are thin, and you can see the oxygen in the alveoli, and it rushes into the pulmonary capillary in which are travelling. The carbon dioxide rushes out, most of it anyway, and the oxygen molecules grab on to the four spots on the red blood cells. (pause) Suddenly, the purplish blue color that you had grown accustomed to becomes bright red. (pause) As you squeeze through the capillary, you notice that again you are getting into larger tunnels and know you are returning to the heart. (pause) You can hear the heart again as you approach smoothly. The noise is deafening as you enter the left atrium — visualize the large chamber. It squeezes and pushes you through the mitral valve into the right ventricle – the ventricle chamber is very large. The "lub dub" is very loud. The ventricle contracts and forces you out through the aortic valve and out through the aorta. Again the pulsing travel is uncomfortable but fun. (pause) You are aware that you are descending down the subclavian artery; you see branches of the artery going off as you again notice that the walls are beginning to get smaller. (pause) As you enter the radial artery and travel down toward the finger, you notice that you are heading toward the capillaries. You see the bright red blood cells around you begin to send their oxygen molecules into the cells and they are immediately replaced by the carbon dioxide molecules from the cells. (pause) The blood turns bluish purple again. (pause) Again the capillaries turn into veins, and you begin to ascend up the arm. The doctors have been tracking you, and you now notice that they have plunged a needle directly ahead into the vein you are in. They begin to pull on the syringe, and they suck you up into it. Feel the suction from the syringe. (pause) From the syringe they eject you into a petri dish. (pause) Exposure to the air, as you open the door to your plastic bubble, automatically makes you grow to your normal size. (pause)

Discussion:

1. What items mentioned in the scenario were difficult to visualize in your mind's eye?
2. Can you imagine your own body with this system?

Variations: Trips through the digestive system, brain, and other systems or metabolic functions would also be appropriate.

Educational Imagery Strategy 5

KING SALMON FISH LIFE CYCLE

Purpose: To reinforce the information given the students regarding the life cycle of the salmon fish. It is assumed that the scenes they are to imagine would have been presented earlier.

Type: Directive; cognitive reinforcing

Monologue: Imagine yourself at the tops of the mountains near a crystal clear, narrow stream. Look around and see the beautiful pine trees, (pause) the tall grass (pause) and winding stream. (pause) Hear the rushing sound of the stream; (pause) see a small salmon egg, orange in color, bouncing its way down stream. Imagine yourself floating over the stream and following the egg down in its journey toward the ocean. (pause) Imagine that a little fish hatches from the egg and begins to swim downstream; (pause) see it eat algae and other plants as it begins to grow. Imagine the stream getting larger and deeper and the fish getting larger. (pause) It arrives at a waterfall, and the fish seems to have fun swimming down the fall. (pause) Imagine that the stream has become a large river and the fish is several inches long. (pause) The river flows into the Pacific ocean, and the salmon fish grows to maturity as you see it swimming in the ocean. (pause) Imagine three years passing and now the fish is very large; (pause) and you can see the fish suddenly start swimming from the ocean toward the river it came out of three years earlier. The current is hard, but it swims hard. (pause) Where the color of the fish was silver, imagine it now changing to bright pink. (pause) Notice a hump forming on the back and jaws becoming hooked. (pause) The fish battles upstream; when it comes to the waterfall it slid down so easily swimming down, it now must jump again and again to fight its way to the top of the falls. (pause) Imagine now, after hundreds of miles, that the king salmon is now in the same small stream where it was hatched. (pause) There are several other fish that have made it also, and they are exhausted and weak. Some of their skin is torn. (pause) The fish you have been following suddenly lays thousands of eggs, similar to the egg you began watching at the beginning. You notice that a male fish near your fish discharges a milt onto the eggs, which fertilizes them. A short time passes, and the fish you have been watching dies, (pause) drifts downstream, (pause) decomposes, (pause) and fertilizes the algae that the little fish that will come later will eat. (pause) Three months pass, and the eggs that were spawned now produce little fish, and the cycle begins again.

Discussion:

1. What were the difficult parts of the scene to imagine?
2. Is the life cycle of the king salmon now clear in your minds?
3. Where are the points along the life cycle that can alter or interrupt the life cycle?
4. Is there anything unique about the life cycle as far as environmental conditions are concerned? Does the change from fresh water to salt water and back again take any kind of an adjustment?

Variations: Any life cycle could be reviewed in this fashion, i.e. tapeworm, butterflies, etc.

Chapter 5

AFFECTIVE IMAGERY IN
DECISION MAKING

DECISION MAKING

- Giving Information about the Decision
- **Clarifying Values, Attitudes, and Emotions — Affective Imagery**
- Looking at Alternative Solutions or Options
- Exploring the Consequences to the Alternatives
- Making and Planning to Implement the Decision
- Implementing and Adhering to the Decision

Educational imagery may find its best home in the process of decision making. This is not to be confused with problem solving where there is a right or wrong outcome, which rightly belongs to the cognitive imagery function. Decision making allows the students (not the teacher) to make the ultimate decision as to what is right and wrong for that individual. To better understand the place where educational imagery, and particularly affective imagery, fits into the decision-making process, a brief look at some of the decision-making models will be helpful.

DECISION MAKING

There have emerged several decision-making models in the last few years, most of which have some elements in common. Hamrick (1980) described a model that included the sequential steps of (1) defining a problem, (2) identifying possible solutions, (3) gathering, validating, processing information, and clarifying values,

46

(4) making a decision, (5) trying out the decision, and (6) evaluating the decision. The Kentucky Department of Education's Alcohol and Drug Education Guide entitled "Making Decisions" (1976) specifies the components of making decisions as (1) recognizing and defining the decision to be made, (2) identifying what is important to you and what you want to attain or accomplish, (3) examining the information you already have and seeking and utilizing new information, (4) assessing the consequences involved in choosing each alternative that is available, (5) ranking available choices, (6) making the decision and evaluating, and (7) making an action plan.

One of the most comprehensive works on decision making in recent years is the work of Janis and Mann (1977), who developed pathway models for their conflict theory of decision making. The strength of this model is the explanation of the multidimensional mental mechanisms within the decision-making process. The decision-making stages, according to Janis and Mann, are similar to other models in that the first stage involves the appraisal of the challenge and asks the question "Are the risks serious if I do not change?" The second state explores alternatives and asks "Is this salient alternative an acceptable means for dealing with the challenge?" and "Have I sufficiently surveyed the available alternatives?" The third stage weighs the alternatives to determine which alternative is best and which meets the requirements of the individual making the decision. Stage four gives the individual time to deliberate about the commitment and whether he or she should really implement the decision, and stage five is "adhering despite negative feedback" (Janis and Mann, 1977). Another perspective, although basically the same as Janis and Mann's stages, is that found in Wheeler and Janis's book *A Practical Guide for Making Decisions.*

Although the process of decision making is much more complicated, the simplified steps aid in developing educational imagery strategies for particular stages in the decision-making process. If we were to find commonalities among the decision-making stages cited above and that would fit into the educational imagery concept, they would include the following steps:

1. A stage that identifies and gives information abþut a problem or decision to be made
2. A stage that clarifies the affective component of the problem or decision
3. A stage that looks at alternative solutions and options to a problem or decision
4. A stage that explores the consequences to the alternative and options
5. A stage that makes the decision and prepares to implement it
6. A stage that focuses on implementing and adhering to the decision

The first stage is a very inclusive stage when considering the traditional role of education and that among many the role of education is still only to diseminate information. The process of truly identifying would include learning some information about the problem or decision to be made, understanding the problem from a conceptual basis, and then examining how the information and concepts fit into other dimensions of living. In other words, how does the cognitive affect the social dimension, spiritual dimension, emotional dimension, biological dimension, and intellectual dimension. The very complex process in step one can be aided with cognitive imagery described in Chapter 4. In this chapter the second stage of dealing with and clarifying the affective components of decision making will be explored.

AFFECTIVE IMAGERY

The term *affective* is an encompassing term that includes attitudes, emotions, values, feelings, etc. and can be better understood by looking at the three main types of imagery that are included within the affective imagery function. The first to be explained is emotional imagery, which explores the emotions as it relates to content area. The second affective imagery strategy is spiritual imagery, which looks at the spiritual dimension itself as well as the spiritual components of the topics within the curriculum. The third area within the affective realm is values clarification imagery, which modifies the procedures of the currently popular values clarification methods.

Emotional Imagery

Using the emotions in imagery can help the student in many ways and accomplish several purposes or objectives. The emotions themselves can be explored, and the students can focus on the particular emotion that is under discussion. Consider Educational Imagery Strategy 6 as an example of emotional imagery focusing on the emotion of anger. (*see* Appendix)

Emotional imagery can also be functional in allowing the student to express the emotions in imagined interpersonal situations. In Strategy 7, it could be assumed that the students had talked about the levels of communication, that a first level of communication would be one of information sharing, the second could be an argumentative, authoritarian, or denial type of communication, a level three would be one of exploring the emotions and pondering true feelings, and a level four could be to communicate at a feeling or self-disclosing level. A "spin off" of this strategy is to have students do role reversals and try to imagine the emotions a significant other would feel when they receive the messages that the student sends. (*see* Educational Imagery Strategy 7, Appendix)

When studying the health dilemmas of special groups of people, it is often beneficial for those who do not have the disabilities or problems to empathize with the frustration and emotions associated with the group under study. Sometimes it is difficult to imagine what it would be like to be poor, handicapped, to live on a reservation, to have diabetes, or to be addicted to drugs. Strategy 8 looks at how the class can attempt to empathize with the disease of alcoholism. (*see* Appendix)

Adding the emotional dimension to a sometimes nonemotional topic can encourage the students to become more involved in the topic. For example, environmental health can sometimes be an unemotional topic unless some effort is made to bring out the emotional side. Educational Imagery Strategy 9 focuses on the general aspects of environmental pollutants. (*see* Appendix)

Spiritual Imagery

The spiritual dimension has been interpreted as having the following components and definitions:

1. Something which gives meaning or purpose to life
2. A set of principles or ethics to live by
3. The sense of selflessness and a feeling for others, a willingness to do more for others than yourself
4. Commitment to God; an Ultimate Concern
5. Perception of what it is that causes the universe to work the way it does
6. Something for which there is no rational explanation; recognition of powers beyond the natural and rational
7. Something that is perceived as being unknown or hazily known; something for which there isn't any easy explanation and so it becomes a matter of faith
8. The most pleasure-producing quality of humans because it's so hard to grasp (Banks, 1980)

The individualized nature of educational imagery allows for the incorporation of the spiritual dimension of being into the classroom. Unquestionably, a country's people whose pledge includes the phrase "one nation under God" are deeply influenced by their spiritual selves. With the contemporary moral issues that face today's youth it seems biased not to consider the spiritual aspects of these issues. There is obvious caution in dealing with the issues. We must recognize that students represent a diversity of backgrounds and religions and that the spiritual dimension means different things to different people. We cannot suddenly combine the church and state, and if we did, the teacher bias would surely show. We must respect the convictions of students, and whether they are athiest, Moslem, Jew, or Christian, we cannot attempt to change them or influence them.

Generally speaking, it seems very difficult for the classroom teacher actually to deal with the spiritual dimension objectively without biasing the perception of students or the discussion in the classroom. Through educational imagery, the concept of spirituality may be treated (1) when the topic itself has spiritual implications, (2) as a component of the decision-making process, and (3) as a spiritual experience itself.

Educational Imagery Strategy 10 includes a topic that carries spiritual implications and has become part of the lay literature as well as a component of death and dying courses and units. The life after death phenomenon is controversial but can be handled objectively as one perspective of the death experience. *(see* Appendix) (For a discussion of the approaches and cautions in working with the phenomenon, see Richardson's "The Life After Death Phenomenon," 1979.)

Perhaps in the decision-making process spiritual imagery is most important in that the result of decisions can either be very positive or negative depending upon the congruence of the decision to personal perceptions of good and bad. Even though there should be no bias when dealing with decision making or the spiritual dimension of being, there should be encouragement to behave in accordance with one's spiritual/value system. Incongruence leads to unhappiness and guilt, so either the behaviors should change or the values should change for harmony and peace.

There is a wide range of decisions that have spiritual overtones. Decisions related to the degree of sexual intimacy, having immunizations, taking drugs, smoking, drinking alcohol, dancing, dating, eating, literature selection, historical readings, music sung and listened to, systems of the body that can be studied, movies seen, marking the driver's license to donate organs, and numerous other topics all have religious or spiritual implications. Strategy 11 demonstrates how the spiritual dimension can be included in a decision-making scenario without bias. The topic will be to determine the degree of physical intimacy the students will allow based on their spiritual perspective. (*see* Appendix)

The last component of spiritual imagery is to have a spiritual experience within itself just to promote that part of living. The appropriateness of this strategy depends upon the importance given the spiritual dimension by the classroom teacher. The essence of the strategy is simple; it is very nondirective and simply allows time for the students to get in touch with their spiritual selves (*see* Educational Imagery Strategy 12, Appendix).

Values Clarification Imagery

Values clarification has been practiced relying on two major perspectives since the widespread acceptance of the method in the classroom several years ago. One perspective is that of Rath et al. (1966), which states that values should be publicly affirmed and acted on, while Shaver and Strong (1976) indicate that values, whether or not students are willing to publicly affirm or act on them, are nevertheless values. Many people have used the former perspective in a methodological sense and actually had the students make public stands on issues, some of which have been controversial in nature. In most instances though, teachers have been sensitive to student positions by generalizing the issues or clarifying by putting the situations that bring out values in the third person or having the students affirm their positions privately.

According to Pearce (1979), the identification and clarification of values is "a process of attempting to state what our standards are and how strongly we feel about them." She notes that it is not an easy process because of the difficulty of putting emotions into words. Shaver and Strong indicate that teachers should be cautious about probing into personal beliefs and emotions relating to personal issues, as opposed to basic democratic issues, simply out of respect for the dignity and privacy of students. On the other hand, Pearce also points out that young people need to determine their values, their commitment to their values, and subsequently to make rational decisions based on those values.

With this caution and also identified need, it becomes apparent that educational imagery can aid in the values clarification process by adapting the method of presentation and personalizing them without threatening the dignity and privacy of students. Some examples will demonstrate the process of modifying values clarification methods into a values clarification imagery strategy merely by having the students imagine the situations rather than discussing them. Examples of moral dilemmas, values voting/ranking, and spread of opinion will be given in this section.

The powerful questions associated with moral dilemmas can be even more effectual if imagery accompanies the moral dilemma. For example, one of several questions developed by Read et al. (1977) is "What would you do if you came across some students smoking pot in the lavatory?" The question expanded into a values clarification imagery strategy would look like Educational Imagery Strategy 13 (*see* Appendix).

Other versions of moral dilemma values clarification strategies involve simple to complex stories that portray several characters in which each behaves in the story to exemplify a selected value.

At the conclusion of the story, the students rank the characters and the values they represent. One of several good qualities of values clarification strategies is that the story is told without personalizing and identifying the characters. If the students were to identify classmates or relatives as the characters in the story, then factors other than the selected values would come into play in the ranking of the characters. There may be times when identifying friends and relatives would be appropriate in a moral dilemma story, and in such a case values clarification imagery would be suitable. In the objective sense, too, imagery can be used to make the story more vivid by imagining the characters and the story. People generally do imagine the story anyway, but the instructor can make the classroom atmosphere more conducive to visualization by preparing the students as described in Chapter 3.

A moral dilemma such as the popular Alligator River (Simon et al., 1972) could have the students visualize the river with the alligators in it and imagine what Abigail, Sinbad, Ivan, Slug, and Gregory would look like. A good discussion could result from the names and the images that were formed in the minds of the students. For example, since Sinbad has a boat and carries a sailor's name, many will imagine Sinbad as a big man with a dark beard, much like a stereotypic pirate. If Sinbad were a frail man, clean shaven, and very polite, it is likely that the value that Sinbad represented would be altered in the ranking with the modified image.

Another moral dilemma approach, first, is to identify numerous characters, that is followed by a decision on the part of the students to give some of the characters a less desirable fate than other characters in the dilemma. For example, some selected characteristics that carry value meanings could be given to fourteen people in a bomb shelter with provisions for only seven people. The students would be assigned the task of forcing seven people out of the shelter. The characteristics the people could have could be religious (priest, rabbi, minister, bishop), racial, professional (doctor, lawyer, policeman) and personal characteristics (drug pusher or user, diabetic, olympic athlete, prostitute, etc.). The sketchy details again can become more vivid using imagery to visualize the individuals in the shelter. Scenarios could be developed that would follow the survivors through interpersonal situations. Educational Imagery Strategy 14 exemplifies a moral dilemma values clarification strategy using imagery as the method of presentation (*see* Appendix).

Another values clarification strategy is to have a Spread of Opinion. The students are given a description of two people, each representing a position on the end of a liberal-conservative continuum: an alcoholic versus a teetotaler, an antismoking activist versus a four pack a day cigarette smoker, a bookworm versus a person who hates to read street signs, a person who has sex just for the kicks versus the celibate are examples of ends of the continuum. Educational Imagery Strategy 15 is a values clarification imagery method using the spread of opinion approach (*see* Appendix).

Values voting and values ranking generally pose a number of value-laden options to the students for which the students are asked to rank or vote for the item or option they most value. Posing the options without imagining the circumstances may result in a different response than when the students place themselves in the situation described by the teacher and even follow through on the outcome of the choice, similar to consequence imagery described in the next chapter. Educational Imagery Strategy 16 elaborates a values voting strategy (*see* Appendix).

The next chapter will describe educational imagery strategies related to the decision-making process that explore the outcomes of solutions or alternative choices.

Appendix
EDUCATIONAL IMAGERY STRATEGIES

Educational Imagery Strategy 6
BOTTLED-UP ANGER

Purpose: To help students reflect on their pent-up feelings and to introduce the discussion of outlets for emotions (in this case, anger).

Type: Directive; emotional

Monologue: Close your eyes and remember a time in your life that you were very angry. Do not think about the circumstances of the experience, only the feeling that you had. Remember how you felt. (pause) Imagine now that your body is like a bottle and that your mouth and nose are the opening to the bottle. If you want to, you can hold everything inside your body, including the emotion of anger. The feeling of anger that you felt earlier, I want you to imagine, is inside your bodily bottle; perhaps you can imagine the feeling as a pulsing mass inside of you. (pause) Hold that anger inside — imagine the pressure inside of you. Sometimes you forget about it, but it is always there! Imagine now that more of the anger mass is entering your body, and the pressure increases, but you continue to hold it in. (pause) Imagine the damage the emotions are doing to your body. (pause) Still another dose of anger and the mass is starting to engulf the whole inside of you, but you still fight to hold it inside. (pause) It makes you cranky — you know that the anger is so strong and that it has to come out, you can feel that it is hurting the inside of your body. Imagine now how you will let that anger out — will you yell, cry, run, laugh, hit, throw? (pause) Now breath deeply and feel how relaxed you are; there is no more pressure. Your bodily bottle is clear and pressure free. Breath deeply and relax.

Discussion:

1. Can you feel the difference in bottling up emotions and allowing them to escape?

2. What kind of effects can keeping anger bottled up have on the body, social life, spiritual life, or the other emotions?
3. What were the ways to release anger? Which are socially acceptable?
4. How important is it to vent anger?

Variations: The other emotions would obviously work in a similar scenario, i. e. what happens to bottled-up love? Using consequence imagery, one could follow the outcomes of good and bad types of anger release.

Educational Imagery Strategy 7
SELF DISCLOSING COMMUNICATION

Purpose: To allow the student to rehearse mentally a feeling level of communication with a loved one.

Type: Nondirective; emotional

Monologue: Imagine someone that you care about very deeply, a parent, another relative, a girl friend, or boyfriend. Visualize the person's hair (if any), the facial outline, (pause) the skin, (pause) the eyes, and see him or her smiling. (pause) Imagine the fragrance about the person. (pause) Imagine a place that you can be alone to talk with that person; it can be real or imaginary; be sure now to sense all the aspects of the environment, see the surroundings, (pause) smell the smells, and hear the sounds of the place. (pause) Now imagine that you are with the person in the environment that you have selected and will now carry on a conversation with that person. Identify an emotion or feeling that you would like to express to the person using self-disclosure and expressing true feelings with good communication techniques. Imagine the other person's responses as well as your own. Complete the scenario.

Discussion:
1. Was it a positive experience?
2. What is the likelihood of the person that you identified responding as he or she did in your scenario?
3. Would it be beneficial in your relationship with this person to actually communicate in this way?
4. How many of you have done in real life what you imagined here?
5. Is there someone else that you should have selected for this scenario?

Variations: Having the students jump from an argumentative level to a feeling level or imagining other conversations at different levels would be beneficial. Assertiveness or anger venting scenarios would also be helpful.

Educational Imagery Strategy 8
ALCOHOLISM EMPATHY

Purpose: To allow the student to reflect upon the emotional dilemmas of the alcoholic.

Type: Directive; emotional

Monologue: You are the same age as you are now, but with the exception that you are a heavy drinker. Imagine that you have learned to use alcohol to bury your problems and worries and you have developed quite a tolerance for drinking. (pause) Assume that you feel that you need four or five drinks a day to feel good. You don't feel that you are an alcoholic but only that the drinks make you feel better and temporarily forget about your problems. The first scenario that I want you to imagine is that you have not had a drink for sometime and you feel very thirsty; imagine how you feel when you haven't had any water for a long time, your mouth is dry and parched, you long for cool water to go down your throat to relieve the thirst, but you just can't have any now. (pause) That same driving force for water will occupy your mind while you are doing regular activities. Imagine doing what you would do after class today, but with this tremendous drive for the drink. You don't want to play, study, or work but only live for that drink. (pause) With unrelenting force, your drive gets so strong that you begin to shake and tremble and get very sick. (pause) Assume time has passed and you have had your drink and much more — you are drunk. Envision being at home with a loved one, someone you now get along with well and love. Imagine the person as clearly as you can — see him or her happy, imagine being with that person, expressing love either verbally, with a hug, or however you are comfortable expressing that love. (pause) Imagine that some force in your drunken state is forcing you to yell uncontrollably at that person when he or she has only asked to help you. (pause) Imagine yelling that you need no help and you call the person names. (pause) Visualize yourself throwing that person down or perhaps striking and hurting him or her. (pause) Imagine the hurt the person feels. (pause) See yourself take some money from the person's wallet or purse, and runing out. (pause) Reflect on those feelings you have when facing that person again and the force no longer compels you to do those things.

Discussion:

1. How hård is it to function and accomplish projects when you have a craving for a drink?
2. Can you understand how sometimes the alcoholic becomes antisocial and irritable?
3. Can you imagine how guilty an alcoholic might feel after doing something uncontrollable?
4. If you know an alcoholic, how can you best help that person?

Variations: The alcoholic may find him/herself in other situations that could be imagined by the student such as incompetence at work or school, not coming home, not enough money for necessities because the money was spent on alcohol, etc., which could serve as other scenarios. Additionally, the health dilemmas of the poor, disabled, the native American on the reservation, the cardiac patient, the epileptic, diabetic, and other dilemmas could be imagined if appropriate to the discussion.

Educational Imagery Strategy 9
BACK TO NATURE

Purpose: To have the students reflect on the devastating effects environmental pollutants can have in nature.

Type: Directive; emotional

Monologue: Close your eyes and imagine a beautiful outdoor scene, either imaginary or an actual place. In this scene I want you to imagine some trees (pause) and water in the form of an ocean, river, stream, or lake. (pause) Imagine the wildlife, such as birds, squirrels, etc. that may be present. (pause) Hear the sounds that should be there: the ripple of the lake, the bubbling of the stream, the pounding of the waves of the ocean, the breezes in the trees. The air is clear, the water is clear, it is a beautiful day. Take a few minutes to enjoy this beautiful place; focus your thoughts on the smells, the colors, the sounds of this beautiful place. (long pause)

Imagine suddenly that there is a road in the distance with bumper to bumper traffic — the air around the road is gray, and it moves over your special place. The sky is no longer clear but gray. Imagine how it would look. (pause) Imagine how it would smell. (pause) Some distance away and near the body of water you are near, imagine a factory beginning to dump wastes into the body of water. Visualize now the crystal clear water becoming murky with bubbles floating, and you can no longer see the bottom. (pause) It is hard to hear the birds now from the honking of the horns and traffic noise; also there is the factory noise. (pause) Imagine, too, that people begin to come to your place with picnic materials. (pause) They play, carve their initials on the trees, (pause) break some of the branches, (pause) throw their paper plates into the water; (pause) half eaten hot dogs are on the ground with other trash. (pause) Reflect on the total scene of your special place. (pause) Complete the scenario now by going through the steps that could be taken to restore the place to its original or optimal state.

Discussion:

1. How did you feel when I began to ruin your beautiful place?
2. Have you seen places that have the same problem?
3. Have you ever imagined how a place that was ruined because of pollution looked before it was ruined?
4. What kind of bias was there in this scenario?
5. How many of the steps that you took to restore the scene were realistic?

Variations: Have the students imagine a local place that is either beautiful, that everyone would recognize, or else have them imagine a place that is eroded, polluted, etc., and imagine what it could be or was like in its virgin state.

Educational Imagery Strategy 10
LIFE AFTER DEATH PHENOMENON

Purpose: To allow the students to visualize from their own perceptions the potential events of death, similar to those described by patients who have had near-death experiences.

Type: Directive; spiritual

Monologue: Today you are going to experience death, not as a terrifying end but as a natural part of life, a transition stage. On my command you will experience death, and at that moment you will see yourself rise to the ceiling of the room and look down upon your own lifeless form. You will die now. (pause) As you look upon your body you are not frightened, just feeling a little awkward in your new state of being. (pause) You are interested but not upset as people try to revive you. You can see loved ones who hear the news of your death and mourn. Try to reassure them that you are content in your new state. Some of them feel your presence and are reassured. (pause) You now return to overlook your body again and look at it for the last time — you hear a buzzing noise; (pause) and with the noise you feel yourself going through a long dark tunnel at a tremendous speed. (pause) As you approach the end of the tunnel you open into a beautiful spot. You see rolling, grassy, meadows; (pause) on the right you see beautiful trees. (pause) On the left is a crystal clear lake. (pause) Some of your favorite animals are at play. Take a few moments to hear the sounds, feel the gentle breeze, and smell the fragrance of this beautiful spot. (pause) In the distance you see people approaching you, and they are singing beautiful songs (taped music is effective here). As they approach, you recognize relatives and friends who have already died. You recognize great grandparents whom you have never seen, perhaps, but know them now. Embrace some of these relatives. (pause) Then there is a hush, and a being of light approaches you. The power of love you feel from this being is over-whelming. You are almost choked up inside and feel tears coming to your eyes, so powerful is the love this being has for you. (pause) The being puts his arms around you, and you almost melt within those strong arms. Enjoy the moment. (pause) This being now communicates with you nonverbally that you will now have a panoramic playback of your whole life from infancy to the present — enjoy that play-back (Note: be sure to allow enough of a pause for this). You are given a choice by the being to stay or return (short pause). You want to stay in the beau-tiful state, but you realize that you have a purpose to fulfill, so you decide to return. Suddenly you are back in your body, alive. (pause) Before opening your eyes, you are struck with a number of feelings. What is surprising is that what seemed like hours has been but a few minutes. More important, you feel a tremendous desire to show, give, and receive love. (pause) Also, you are impressed with a need to seek knowledge in all its forms.

Discussion:

1. How many were able to visualize the experiences of this scenario?
2. Do you feel death could be as wonderful as the scenario? Explain.
3. Are there good reasons for people to have near-death experiences?
4. Do you think a suicide or violent death would yield as pleasant an experience? Explain.
5. What can we learn in relation to our life-styles from people who have had these types of experiences?

Variations: Using a suicidal situation, students could have a neg-ative experience reliving problems that caused them to commit suicide.

Educational Imagery Strategy 11
THE SPIRITUAL SIDE OF PHYSICAL INTIMACY

Purpose: To help students who are not married to make choices regarding physical intimacy and include the spiritual dimension in their decision.

Type: Nondirective; spiritual

Monologue: Imagine for a moment a spiritual scenario such as talking to a spiritual mentor, such as a religious leader or God, praying, meditating, communing with nature, or other scenario that focuses on your spiritual being. During this scenario, get as close emotionally to the source of your spiritual strength as you can. Feel the emotions of the scenario. (pause) During this time, communicate nonverbally or verbally with the source and decide the degree of physical intimacy that would make you comfortable to be able to return to the spiritual state. (pause)

— discussion here for complete break —

Break for a moment and imagine yourself with someone with whom you are currently emotionally involved or a fantasy/movie star type of person with whom you could imagine being emotionally involved. (pause) Look at all the details of that person; imagine him or her smiling; (pause) smell the fragrance the person has that makes you almost melt when you are close to him or her. (pause) Imagine a place to be with that person alone, a place that is comfortable for you. (pause) Imagine touching hands, (pause) being close; enjoy this for a moment. (pause) Complete the scenario, a whole evening if you wish, visualizing, in addition to other things, how physically intimate you will become with that person, based on the decision made in the earlier spiritual scenario. (pause) Imagine that the partner you are with decides to become more intimate than you have decided and becomes persuasive to be

more intimate. (pause) Imagine how you will deal
with the situation and still have a pleasant evening.

Discussion:

1. Were you able to have a spiritual experience?
2. Were you able to decide at that time the degree
   of physical intimacy that is spiritually comfortable?
3. Was there any dissonance between the behavioral
   expectations of the first scenario and the second
   scenario?
4. Should the two be congruent?

Variations: In the romantic scenario, have the students go beyond their decision made in the first spiritual scenario and then return to the spiritual scenario and
discuss the issue of congruence of the spiritual dimensions and guilt.

The second scenario can involve a range of other
choices such as drug-taking behavior, alcohol con-
sumption, honesty, etc.

Educational Imagery Strategy 12
TUNING IN

Purpose: To have the student get in touch with or reinforce the importance of the spiritual dimension of being.

Type: Nondirective, spiritual

Monologue: Identify and imagine your source of spiritual strength, perhaps in nature, in the cosmos, in God, Jesus Christ, or other religious mentor. Imagine first meeting with that essence, enjoying a relationship, and sharing with the source the things that you want to share. Experience the emotion of this occasion. Imagine the life-style you want to lead based on this encounter.

Discussion:

1. How can this type of experience help you in daily living?
2. Is it a beneficial experience?

Variation: The nature of the spiritual could be more directive if there were some common elements to each class member's spiritual reference, e. g. if all were Christian.

Educational Imagery Strategy 13
POT AT SCHOOL

Purpose: To have students explore their values related to seeing someone smoking pot illegally.

Type: Nondirective; values clarification imagery

Monologue: Imagine that it is your lunch period and you decide to go to the bathroom alone. Imagine as clearly as you can the bathroom that you would go to. (pause) Imagine the door that enters into the bathroom; see yourself approaching the door, (pause) opening it, and walking in. As you walk in you sense the smell of marijuana; imagine how it smells (if you do not know, then guess what it might smell like). (pause) Look around and see the bathroom as you remember it. (pause) There are three people huddled in the corner. Imagine three people whose names you might know who might be smoking marijuana. (pause) You can see clearly that they are smoking pot; you recognize the rolled joints. Complete the scenario and do what you would actually do in this situation.

Discussion:
1. What were the options of things you could do in this scenario?
2. Would you really do what you imagined?
3. What would the repercussions of your actions be, if any?
4. Was everybody deserving of the result of your actions?

Variations: The students could be close friends, teachers, or change the scenario to students of the opposite sex. Changing the scene away from the school grounds or at a football game in the evening may change the situation. (For a whole series of questions that trigger scenarios, see Read et al., 1977.)

Educational Imagery Strategy 14
SLUMBER PARTY

Purpose: To allow the students to clarify values related to parental trust, discipline, rough external individuals but with basic values, moral facades, etc. (geared toward junior high school students)

Type: Nondirective; values clarification

Monologue: Debbie had decided to have a slumber party at her home with some girls; imagine what Debbie would look like. (pause) Imagine a home that would be a place to have the slumber party. If you are a girl, imagine being part of the slumber party; if a male, observe from a distance. Imagine the setting of a slumber party: beds, blankets, pillows, sleeping bags, stereos, tables with food set up for midnight snacks in the den. Although there are several girls, I want you to identify two others at the party, Lisa and Cheryl. Lisa talks as though she is almost a saint; try to imagine her features as she makes statements such as "I don't even kiss boys until I'm sure they love me" and "I won't let one have "roamin' " hands until we're married." Imagine Lisa. (pause) Cheryl, on the other hand, laughs at Lisa, tells her she is old fashioned. They don't argue but tease each other. Cheryl uses poor grammar, profanes with almost every other word, and talks as though she sleeps with anyone she feels like. (pause) Debbie likes both Cheryl and Lisa in different ways. Debbie balances out both of the other girls, has a level head. (pause) Imagine several girls talking this way at the party when suddenly there is a knock on the window. There are two boys whom everyone knows. (pause) Debbie knows that her parents would not want her to have the boys in, but most of the girls want them in. Debbie concedes, even though she knows that her folks don't want them in. Imagine letting the boys in. (pause) Cheryl tells them to leave and that they will cause problems. The boys laugh at her. One of the boys (Mike) is Lisa's boyfriend. Since the other boy (Eric) is doing most of the talking, Mike and Lisa sneak out of the room. Debbie's parents, hearing male voices, come to the door of the room where the slumber party is going on. Imagine that as the parents are entering, Eric ducks under some sleeping bags. The parents ask where the male voices came from. (pause) Debbie denies that there were any. Cheryl, on the other hand, says "Don't lie" and pulls the sleeping bag off Eric. (pause) The parents ask if that is the only boy. Cheryl says no and goes to the next room where Lisa and Mike are semi-nude embracing. The parents send all the girls home and "ground" Debbie for three months.

Visualize the individuals and rank in order the parents, Debbie, Lisa, Cheryl, Mike, and Eric, from the least objectionable character to the most objectionable character.

Discussion:

1. What characteristics do the individuals in the story represent?
2. Do you still rate the characteristics the same as you did the people?
3. Why is it important to rank these; what life-styling implications does this have?

Variations: Other characteristics would make the story different depending on the topic. Drugs could be introduced in the story, an overweight junk food junkie, smoking, or homosexuality.

Educational Imagery Strategy 15
EUSTRESS OR DISTRESS

Purpose: To allow the students to evaluate themselves relative to eustressful and distressful life-styles.

Type: Nondirective; values clarification imagery

Monologue: Imagine a person of your same sex who is very sensitive to his or her stress levels and practices all kinds of stress management strategies. First imagine the person's physical appearance. (pause) Now imagine that person practicing meditation. (pause) Visualize the person planning a day according to priorities. (pause) Imagine that person eating a balanced (low sugar, low salt, no coffee or colas) meal. Visualize that person jogging. (pause) Visualize that person being assertive in the classroom when appropriate. Imagine the person saying no to an unnecessary activity because he or she has too much to do. (pause) Imagine the person altering goals because some are unrealistic, e. g. he or she cannot be a cheerleader so is trying out for an athletic team or choir. (pause) Change the person and this time imagine someone of the same sex who does not care about stress. (pause) Imagine the person's features. (pause) Imagine the person waking up sleepy because he or she stayed up so late watching TV. (pause) See how nervous he or she is going to school with only partially completed homework. (pause) Visualize the person playing raquetball, losing, but determined to win and cursing because he or she makes mistakes. (pause) Imagine the person always looking at his or her watch, trying toward perfection. (pause) Visualize the food the person eats: sweet rolls and coffee for breakfast, white bread sandwiches and colas for lunch. (pause)

Now imagine yourself doing activities similar to one of these people. Imagine your life-style, related

to stress, someplace on a continuum between the
two people you have just imagined.

Discussion:

1. What were the good and the bad characteristics
of each of the life-styles?
2. As you painted your ideal life-style, how realistic
was it? Is there a reason not to implement the life-
style now?

Variations: Other extremes as mentioned in the text can be employed: sexually free versus sexually conservative,
honest versus dishonest, positive attitudes toward
old age versus negative stereotyping, etc.

Educational Imagery Strategy 16
CHOOSING AND LIVING WITH VALUES

Purpose: To have the students identify what they value from selected choices and then live with the choices to understand and clarify why they made the choice.

Type: Nondirective; value/clarification imagery (modified values voting/ranking)

Monologue: Suppose that you are suddenly shipwrecked and stranded on a deserted island. There is plenty of food and water, but you will probably have to stay on the island for several months, maybe a year, before help comes. Sit down on the beach. (pause) Feel the warm white sand. (pause) Smell the sea breeze; (pause) hear the rustling of the palm trees. Feel the warm sun on your body. (pause) During the shipwreck you recall that you had three books; one was a book that is the basis of your religion or spiritual domain (such as the Bible), the second book was a book on survival and living in the wilderness, and the third was a comprehensive work on the history of civilization. As you look out over the beach, you see washed up on the shore one of the books in a water-tight plastic bag. Imagine racing down and getting the book; which do you hope it will be? (pause) Complete a scenario of your lifestyle on the island using that book you have selected as a source of support or diversion. (pause)

After a couple of days, you look out over the waves and see a life raft with one person on it paddling in towards the beach — who in all the world do you hope is on it to keep you company? (pause) Imagine that person joining you and the life-style you would lead with him/her. (pause)

Imagine that there were only four kinds of food on the island. Imagine eating the four foods and they are the four foods you would pick to live on for a year. (pause)

Discussion:

    1. Were you entertained or did you develop yourself with the literature that you chose?

    2. Having acted out the situation in your mind, would you change your choice?

    3. Was the person you selected a support person or a companionship relationship? In what way was your life-style different with that person than if you had been at home?

    4. Was the food you selected nutritious, balanced?

    5. Can you imagine your health status after a year? Would it be good based on your selection?

Variations: Any number of values situations could be presented in this scenario. Other situations would also force a person to make choices, such as a plane crash in the mountains, cave-in, etc. Ranking of the scenario can add to the valuing, i. e. a second book, second person, more foods, etc.

Chapter 6

CONSEQUENCE IMAGERY IN DECISION MAKING

DECISION MAKING

- Giving Information about the Decision
- Clarifying Values, Attitudes, and Emotions
- Looking at Alternative Solutions or Options
- **Exploring the Consequences to the Alternatives — Consequence Imagery**
- Making and Planning to Implement the Decision
- Implementing and Adhering to the Decision

After the dissemination of information has occurred, students should have clarified their values and should be prepared to explore alternative solutions related to a problem, behavior, or decision. The next step in the decision-making process is to allow the students to brainstrom and arrive at several alternatives. Every possible alternative to the problem should be considered when brainstorming to promote awareness. For example, a student has a friend who, unbeknown to significant others, is using hard drugs. This leaves the student to contemplate a decision regarding his/her action or inaction regarding the friend. The list of alternatives for the student would be to approach the authorities, parents, or clergy; do absolutly nothing and ignore it; talk to the friend and try to persuade him to get help; and other logical approaches to the problem. With brainstorming, illogical and unethical alternatives should also surface as more extreme approaches, such as

75

"hog-tieing" the friend until he/she is over withdrawal, encouraging him/her to continue to use the drug, joining in taking drugs, tampering with the drugs the friend is taking such as replacing the drug with milk sugar, and other wild ideas. Students will be even more creative with responses in a brainstorming situation, and among the ideas will surface a few good alternatives.

The purpose of consequence imagery is to select two or three of the most viable options resulting from the brainstorming and mentally follow the scenarios to determine what would happen if the students actually performed the option. The students imagine each of the viable options as clearly as they can, live through the consequences as they would probably occur, then based on the outcomes of the scenarios, the choice becomes clearer. How long to follow the consequence ranges from immediate responses to alternatives to following the consequences of the choices for several years, depending upon the nature of the topic. If the scenario about the drug user were used, it would be important to follow the life-style of the user and the student for several years after the student's action or lack of action, exploring guilt feelings perhaps, immediate peer rejection, health problems, and other dimensions of the problem. The outcomes of all types of decisions can be aided through simple consequence imagery, which is to follow the outcomes of a single decision. Educational Imagery Strategies 17 and 18 are examples of consequence imagery (*see* Appendix).

Consequence imagery can be used in more complex situations where one decision can lead to another decision, which leads to another decision, and so forth. This type of consequence imagery is called *progressive consequence imagery* and leaves much for the student to imagine and should be used when the students are quite competent in imagery and able to follow the scenarios on their own. The students in progressive consequence imagery must be able to jump into a scenario, break for discussion, then jump back into the scenario to complete the outcome of the initial decisions.

The stages of progressive consequence imagery are as follows:
1. Lead into the first decision-making scenario.
2. Break for students to discuss the possible outcomes and alternatives of the first decision.
3. Students follow the two or three best choices through imagery until they face another decision.

4. The students break for discussion to explore the alternatives of the second decision.
5. The students follow the viable alternatives until another decision is made. The process continues for each decision encountered.

The following diagram represents the paths that could be followed in consequence imagery. If all the paths were followed, it would be a very long session.

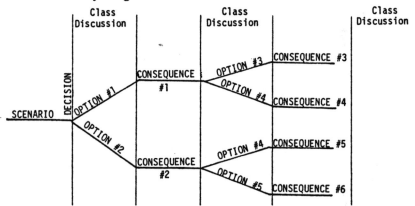

Progressive consequence imagery obviously cannot follow too many decisions without becoming very complex. By making two successive decisions and assuming each decision has only two viable alternatives, six scenarios must be followed in addition to the initial scenario. If three successive decisions were to be made then there would be fourteen total consequences to follow, which is very burdensome for a classroom situation but could certainly be done on an individual basis.

When students are competent with educational imagery, they can be encouraged to follow the outcomes of several successive decisions without needing to follow discarded options. This necessitates allowing the students to create their own scenarios without teacher direction except on the first decision. It is a good idea for the teacher to stop periodically though for discussion and let students know where others are in the progression. The following diagram shows the path that an individual might take during an individualized progressive imagery strategy. The solid lines represent the path that an individual student may take, and the dotted lines represent the path that others in the class may take.

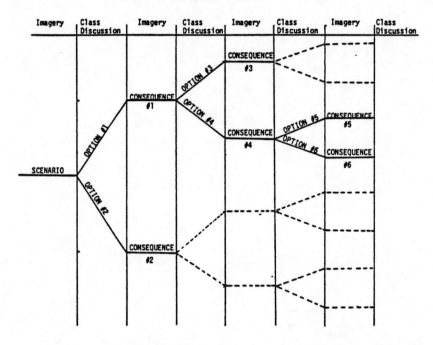

There are many subjects that are conducive to progressive consequence imagery. An example might be in parenting education where the progressive choices would be to get married or not, to have children or not, to use spanking as a punishment or not, and on through parenthood. This line of thinking would be making an affirmative choice among the alternatives. The other path of this situation would be to get married or not, to live with a partner or not, to have affairs or not, etc. Educational Imagery Strategy 19 is an example of progressive consequence imagery (*see* Appendix).

The next chapter deals with the incorporation of decisions into one's life-style. Simulation imagery aids in the final step of the decision-making process.

Appendix

EDUCATIONAL IMAGERY STRATEGIES

Educational Imagery Strategy 17
CRASH

Purpose: To let students explore the consequences of buck-ling their seatbelts when riding in a car versus not buckling their seatbelts.

Type: Directive; consequence imagery

Monologue: Imagine yourself riding in the car with someone else driving (identify who that person is) and you are on the passenger side. Imagine the car you would be driving. (pause) Look at the color of the interior, (pause) what the person driving might be wearing. Imagine fastening your seat belt and shoulder strap, and the driver does also. (pause) As you visualize this scenario, imagine looking at the driver; suddenly panic comes over his/her eyes and he/she slams on the brake. The car had been going 50 miles per hour. You hear the screech of tires and then a collision, feel the jolt of the impact as you stop quickly, feel the shoulder strap pull at your shoulder and the belt strap pull against the force of your body. (pause) The front of the car is smashed, but you and your driver, although shaken up, are unhurt. (pause)

Modify the scenario now by letting the belt and shoulder strap go unbuckled. (pause) Imagine your-self in the same car with the same driver, talking. (pause) Again you see the fear come across the driver's face and you see him or her hit the brake. (pause) You hear the sound of the impact, and you see the driver plunge forward. (pause) You see the steering wheel column plunge into his or her stom-ach (pause) and see his/her head flying into the windshield. (pause) Hear the sound of shattering glass as the driver's head hits the windshield and bounces back, bleeding severely. You can feel your-self uncontrollably flying to the front of the car; (pause) you have nothing to grab onto as you feel the thud on your head as you hit the glass. It shatters your skeletal system so that you feel as though it has shattered your head. (pause) The shattered glass falls all around you. (pause) The pain is excruciating as you see blood streaming down from your face; (pause) you can hardly breathe from the blow of your chest on the dashboard. Imagine blacking out.

Discussion:

1. Unfortunately, there are only two alternatives in an accident — either you have a seatbelt on or off. Do you think these two situations are realistic?
2. What are the reasons for people not using seatbelts?
3. Are the reasons worth going through something like the second scenario?

Variations: The accident could have been more descriptive of the situations, seeing an approaching car, someone jumping in front of the car, getting rear ended, or rolling over. More emphasis could have been placed on the bothersome nature of the seatbelt for less bias.

Educational Imagery Strategy 18
GOING TOGETHER

Purpose: To help students explore the consequences of going steady or not going steady.

Type: Nondirective; consequence imagery

Monologue: Imagine a person of whom you now are very fond, or if there is no one of whom you are now fond, imagine a "fantasy" person, someone with whom the thought of being with is very inviting. (pause) Focus on the features of that person, the hair, (pause) the eyes, (pause) the facial features, (pause) the figure or physique, and what the person could be wearing. (pause) Picture in your mind the lifestyle you would lead if you were to "go with" that person and only that person. Think of all the positive aspects of that arrangement. Consider how good it feels not to worry about getting dates; (pause) feel the security (pause) and other positive aspects you can imagine. Imagine yourself at a party; picture a place, (pause) people, (pause) and activity (pause). Sense how comfortable it is to have a steady to be with. (pause) Imagine now the negative aspects of going with that person, such as limited acquaintances of the opposite sex, (pause) labeling as "his girl" or "her guy;" (pause) imagine seeing someone you would like to go out with but cannot, (pause) and feel the emotions of eventually "breaking up." (pause)

Change the scene now to being with the same person but not going together. Imagine all the good things about not making a commitment of dating only that person. Think perhaps of being able to "play the field," getting to know many members of the opposite sex as intimately as you want while still dating the one in the first scenario; (pause) sense the freedom, the new challenges. (pause) Complete the scenario looking at the positive aspects of the life-style. Go to the same party with the freedom of "playing the field." (pause) Now think of the negative aspects of not going steady, such as worrying about getting dates, (pause) insecurity (pause). Finish the scenario by visualizing situations that would be negative by not having a steady.

Discussion:

1. Would the decision be harder with a not so ideal "steady"?
2. If the person has shortcomings, how does that complex the scenes?
3. Logically, and avoiding the emotional factor, which seems to be the best between dating around and getting to know one person very well?

Variations: A simpler version might be to create two identical scenarios (such as the party) and then to have one as going steady and one not going steady.

Educational Imagery Strategy 19
VENEREAL DISEASE CHOICES

Purpose: To allow students to explore the consequences of an encounter with someone who has syphilis.

Type: Nondirective; progressive consequence imagery

Monologue: Imagine that you have had a sexual encounter with someone who has syphilis. You did not know it at the time. Many of you would never have sexual encounters because of your values, but we are going to assume that it has happened. Imagine the initial symptoms; the chancre appears on you; it doesn't hurt. (pause) Imagine with as much detail as you can the steps that you would take to get a diagnosis; imagine where you would go.

NOTE: At this point there would be a class discussion of places to go for treatment and disgnosis, or another option would be not to go for treatment at all. Suppose the class came up with the two options of not doing anything and going to a clinic for diagnosis. The second step in the progressive imagery is to follow the first option, and the third step is to follow the second option.

The alternative that we are going to follow first is the option not to do anything but hope the disease will pass. Imagine that in a few weeks the chancre goes away, and you feel relieved. (pause) After several weeks you notice that you are getting a skin rash; it covers your whole stomach area. (pause) Visualize the rash disappearing. Several years are passing without recurrence. Unbeknownst to you, the spirochete had burrowed into various tissues, the blood vessels, the central nervous system, and the bones. (pause) Feel yourself becoming blind; gradually you lose your vision (pause). Feel yourself losing your sense of balance, becoming clumsy. (pause) You find yourself becoming mentally deficient. You no longer are mentally stable, and will have to be committed to a state institution. (pause) Still at a young age, you have a heart attack, and you die. (pause)

Change the scene to the other option of getting treatment. Imagine going to a clinic; imagine how you feel as you walk in the door. (pause.) Tell the receptionist of your need and the symptoms you have had and that you still have the chancre. (pause) Imagine getting the Wasserman blood test; imagine how it feels. (pause) Hear the nurse inform you that you have syphilis. (pause) Imagine getting the penicillin shots; see the syringe; imagine how it feels. (pause) Imagine now the question that you are asked, "Whom did you contact to get the syphilis? Will you give me their name?" Do you tell the nurse or not? Do you call the person? What will you do?

NOTE: Again, a break in the scenario would allow the class to talk about the two options, telling or not, and then go into the outcome of each decision.

What would happen if you told the nurse? Imagine the nurse calling the contact. (pause) Imagine with as much detail as you can the resulting conversation you have with the person face to face.

Change the scenario now and imagine what would happen to the person if you did not tell. Imagine them going through what you perhaps experienced in the first situation, without treatment. (pause)

Discussion:
1. What is the best option of all of these?
2. How could the first situation not ever happen?
3. How did you imagine the partner reacting to the news of disease?

Variations: Other alternatives could have included parental involvement, the students could have been informed of the disease from the partner, and choices of where to go for treatment could have been expanded, such as going to a "quackery clinic."

Chapter 7

SIMULATION IMAGERY IN DECISION MAKING

DECISION MAKING

• Giving Information about the Decision

• Clarifying Values, Attitudes, and Emotions

• Looking at Alternative Solutions or Options

• Exploring the Consequences to the Alternatives

• **Making and Planning to Implement the Decision — Simulation Imagery**

• Implementing and Adhering to the Decision

Simulation imagery functions in a general sense for all types of educational imagery described in this book. To simulate implies that the student conjures an image in his or her mind that approximates the way a situation actually is or would be. Much like simulation games that mimic courtrooms, city council meetings, and other situations, simulation imagery mimics situations in which a behavior will be enacted, a decision will be made, or an emotion experienced. In this sense, readiness imagery, consequence imagery, affective imagery, life-style imagery, and other types of imagery, in some instances, use simulation imagery as a means of accomplishing their primary function.

Within the decision-making format, simulation imagery functions to create a scenario in the mind of the student that provides an opportunity to rehearse and incorporate the decision that the student has made. The decision or behavioral implementation is

86

based upon the previous steps in the decision-making process. The student should have gathered ample information, explored and clarified values and attitudes, looked at alternative solutions, explored the consequences of those alternatives, and then made the choice. The situation(s) that the student imagines will help him/her to see how the decision will affect his/her life in a positive sense.

The two approaches to simulation imagery are progressive simulation imagery and situational simulation imagery. Progressive simulation imagery is nondirective and very individualistic in that the student selects specific behaviors related to the course content and systematically implements the behaviors through imagery, imagining the situations in which they will be incorporated. Examples of behaviors that are conducive to progressive simulation imagery are beginning a fitness program, quitting smoking or drinking, developing social skills, changing attitudes, becoming more studious, or other multisituational behaviors. The student in progressive simulation imagery envisions several scenarios where the behavior could be enacted and progresses from one scenario to another over time, generally from the present to future scenarios. Educational Imagery Strategy 20 exemplifies a progressive simulation imagery strategy (*see* Appendix).

SITUATIONAL SIMULATION IMAGERY

Situational simulation imagery provides the students an opportunity to make either informed or impromptu decisions as they react to a teacher-directed scenario. The students are guided into a situation to which most students can relate, then given a choice to make an action decision. This differs from the progressive simulations in that the student does not create the scenarios or pre-plan the enactment of the decision. Instead he/she becomes a victim of the situation and then acts mentally as he/she would if actually in the situation. The action is based on previous information, clarified values, and exploring the consequences of alternatives. Educational Imagery Strategies 21, 22, and 23 exemplify the situational simulation imagery strategy (*see* Appendix).

Situational simulation imagery is also effective in the liberal arts to empathize with characters in history or in literature. Taking the students through a scenario in the battle of Gettysburg, where they could assume the role of generals plotting strategy, leading up to critical points such as Pickett's Charge is effective. In the book *Oliver Twist,* perhaps the students could assume the role of Oliver and make decisions based on the events of the book, then read ahead to see if the decisions they made conformed with the decisions made by Oliver. Educational Imagery Strategy 24 functions as a situational simulation imagery strategy to empathize with the decisions related to the taking of the Alamo (*see* Appendix).

COMBINING SIMULATION IMAGERY WITH CONSEQUENCE IMAGERY

It is very effective in many cases to combine simulation imagery with consequence imagery for a very powerful efficacious strategy. The student is usually guided into a situational simulation scenario, given the opportunity to make the decision in that situation and then to follow the outcome of the decision. For example, Educational Imagery Strategy 25 dealing with the degree of physical intimacy before marriage has proven effective in weighing the consequences of alternatives presented in a simulation format (*see* Appendix).

Chapter 8 describes the use of educational imagery in adapting one's life-style to a desired ideal entitled life-styling imagery. Additionally, using imagery to improve and rehearse psychomotor skills will also be described.

Appendix

EDUCATIONAL IMAGERY STRATEGIES

Educational Imagery Strategy 20

BECOMING ASSERTIVE

Purpose: To help students to enact their decision to become more assertive.

Type: Directive; progressive simulation imagery

Monologue: Imagine a scene where you wish you were more assertive, a scene where you are generally meeting new people, perhaps the first day of school in a classroom. We will have you repeat the scenario several times, each time becoming more assertive.

Visualize as clearly as you can the situation we just asked you to create. See the environment, (pause) the people around you, (pause) perhaps the noise of many people talking. (pause) Put yourself into the picture, not saying anything perhaps. You want to go over to talk to a group of people but are a little too timid to do it. (pause) Now visualize yourself going over, overcoming your fear, and greeting the other people standing together. (pause) Repeat the scene, and in addition to greeting others, make some compliments, meaningful compliments. (pause) Repeat the scene and make some "I" statements, that is, imagine a conversation that is going on that is interesting to you, and make a statement beginning with "I think." (pause) Imagine someone saying to you that he or she does not agree with you and you ask why. (pause) Share your feelings with someone, when appropriate in the group; imagine clearly doing that. (pause) Imagine a scenario now where you disagree with someone and actually verbalize your disagreement. (pause)

Discussion:

1. What was most difficult for you to do?
2. Would you be able to rehearse this on your own enough to do it?
3. What were the reactions of people to your assertiveness. Was it a positive or negative reaction?

4. Did it feel better to let your position be made
   known or would you rather have left it inside?

Variations: Other social skills and a variety of other situations
for assertiveness could be given (work, home, etc.).

Educational Imagery Strategy 21
FIRE ESCAPE

Purpose: To have students rehearse mentally and become prepared to escape from their home were it to catch on fire.

Type: Nondirective; situational simulation

Monologue: Close your eyes and imagine yourself in your bedroom in your sleeping attire. (pause) Imagine your attire, your room, where your clothes are stored, some features of your room. (pause) You are tired and are crawling into bed and you can feel the warmth of the blankets as you pull the blankets up around you. (pause) As you lie there getting ready to sleep, you can feel yourself starting to get drowsy. (pause) In your sleepy state you smell smoke. You are not alarmed; your thoughts are casual as you ponder the source of the smoke. Look at your closed bedroom door and visualize smoke pouring under the door. (pause) Walk over to the door; feel it — it is hot. (pause) Take a few moments to visualize your move to safety; imagine the steps you would take to get out of your home, carrying what you most value, and perhaps warning those you love without endangering yourself.

Discussion: 1. Were you able to get out of the home?
2. Did you warn others?
3. Did you open the hall door?
4. Could you warn everybody?
5. Do you need to make some adjustments around the home to be better prepared in case of fire?

Variations: Tornado and hurricane preparation would also be beneficial.

Educational Imagery Strategy 22
POT

Purpose: To have students mentally respond as they would to an offer to smoke marijuana.

Type: Nondirective; simulation imagery

Monologue: Imagine yourself with a good friend; visualize that friend. (pause) Imagine doing what you like to do best with that friend. (pause) You can clearly see your surroundings. Take a moment to visualize the things around you, hear the sounds and smell the smells associated with the place you like to be with your friend. (pause) Imagine now you and your friend talking about what you like to talk about alone; if others were around, they leave. (pause) You are sure no one is around as your friend (perhaps very surprisingly) brings out a marijuana joint. You recognize it as marijuana, and your friend, perhaps surprisingly (if this is the first time), attempts to persuade you to smoke it. (pause) The friend encourages the way that only your best friend knows how to persuade you. (pause) The friend then lights up and takes a puff from the marijuana cigarette (pause) and now in your mind you can see the friend extending an arm with the joint for you to take a turn. (pause) Whether you have smoked before or not, this is the first time after you have gone through the decision-making process about marijuana smoking that you have the chance to enforce your decision. If you smoke it, imagine doing it. If you decide not to smoke, imagine how you will say no to your friend but still remain good friends. (pause) Enjoy the rest of the evening with your friend with or without the marijuana.

Discussion:

1. Do you feel good about your decision?
2. Was it a wise choice?

3. Do you think you would make the same decision
   in an actual case?

Variations: Some students may have trouble visualizing a friend
making an offer. This may be introduced by having
the students identify an acquaintance who may or
may not smoke marijauna. Another variation would
be to have a group of peers offer the student a joint.

Educational Imagery Strategy 23
THE TWO YEAR OLD TANTRUM

Purpose: As a function of a parenting class, students will face one of the challenges of being the parent of a two year old. Students will enact decisions they have made regarding discipline of young children.

Type: Nondirective; situational simulation imagery

Monologue: Now that you have a philosophy of discipline, I want you to close your eyes and imagine that you are now a parent of a two year old child. Imagine how your child might look; it can be a boy or a girl. (pause) Imagine how you would feel toward that child. (pause) Imagine hugging and caressing the child and the child responding. (pause) Change the scene now and visualize yourself in a grocery store, a large supermarket. (pause) Imagine that you have a basket full of groceries. Your child has elected to ride in the bottom of the cart. (pause) You have enjoyed being with your child. Visualize passing the candy section on your way to the checkout stand. (pause) Smell the candy. Your child asks for some candy. (pause) You explain that he/she can't have any candy now and you proceed to the checkout stand. (pause) Your child suddenly leaps out of the bottom of the cart and begins to cry for candy. You encourage the child to come along. The child is uncontrollably screaming and stomping his/her feet on the floor. (pause) No matter what you do, the child continues to throw the tantrum. Visualize everyone looking at you. (pause) There are three carts ahead of you in the checkout line. Complete the scenario.

Discussion:

1. What did some of you do? Let's list on the board some of the different things that could have been done.
2. Is this a realistic scenario?

3. Have you seen this happen to people?
4. Do you think of these kinds of scenes when you think about becoming a parent?

Variations: Having both a one and a three year old child compounds the problem when both have a tantrum. The scene could be in a church meeting, at a friend's house, etc.

Educational Imagery Strategy 24

REMEMBER THE ALAMO

Purpose: To help the students to identify with the difficult decision that faced the men and women of the Alamo, the decision between loyalty and patriotism versus their own lives. (geared to junior high school students)

Type: Nondirective; situational simulation imagery

Monologue: Whether you are male or female, imagine yourself as a male volunteer at the Alamo in 1836. For ten days, since February 23, when Colonel William Barret Travis answered Mexican General Antonio Lopez de Santa Anna's surrender ultimatum with a cannon shot, you and the other defenders have withstood the onslaught of an army that ultimately numbered 5,000 men. As you look around, you see 188 others, such as the thirty-two men and boys from Gonzales, other colonists, and the famous Tennessee boys with their leader, Davy Crockett. (pause) As you look over the area you see a large courtyard with large walls in front of the old mission. (pause) The men have gathered together to hear Colonel Travis during one of the lulls in the virtually incessant bombardment. Listen to him tell you about the hopelessness of not getting reinforcements. (pause) The emotion causes his voice to tremble as he tells you that "we cannot win;" he unsheaths his sword and draws a line on the ground in front of you and he states, "Those prepared to give their lives in freedom's cause, come over to me." You are very tired, your eyes are heavy, you don't know how much fight you have left. You know the ammunition and supplies are almost exhausted. See that the men begin to cross the line over to Travis. You see Colonel James Bowie, stricken with typhoid-pneumonia, carried over on his cot. One man decided to surrender; what are you going to do? Consider yourself facing this cause. Is it worth your life? Complete your actions.

Discussion:

1. Would you have the same feelings today?
2. Were men more patriotic then or now?

Variations: It may be beneficial to complete the scenario by saying, "If you chose to stay, or if you only observe, witness the following happening of March 6, 1836.

It is a chilly, predawn morning. Listen to the bugles sounding the dreaded "Deguello" (no quarter to the defenders). Visualize columns of Mexican soldiers attacking from the north, the east, the south, and the west. Imagine twice repulsing them by withering musket fire and cannon shot. They concentrate a third attack at a battered north wall and storm the Alamo.

See Travis, with a single shot through his forehead, fall across his cannon. The Mexicans swarm through the breach and into the plaza. At frightful cost they fight their way to the "Long Barrack" and blast its massive doors with cannon shot. Its defenders, asking no quarter and receiving none, are put to death with grapeshot, musket fire, and bayonets.

Crockett, using his rifle as a club, falls as the attackers, now joined by reinforcements who storm the south wall, turn to the chapel. The Texans inside soon suffer the fate of their comrades. Bowie, his pistols emptied, his famous knife bloodied, and his body riddled, dies on his cot. Mrs. Dickerson, her child, and fourteen other noncombatants who sought refuge here are spared. As you look around you see Santa Anna, minimizing his losses, which numbered nearly 1,600. He says, "It was but a small affair" and orders the bodies of the heroes burned. Colonel Juan Almonte notes the great number of casualties, declares "Another such victory and we are ruined."

Educational Imagery Strategy 25

PARKING

Purpose: To have students make a decision regarding the degree of physical intimacy they feel good about in a dating situation and follow the consequences of the decision.

Type: Nondirective; consequence simulation

Monologue: Imagine that you are out on a date with your favorite person, someone you care about very much. This person may be real and an ongoing relationship or it may be a person of fantasy, the ideal "catch." (pause) Visualize that person very clearly with all his or her features; you can also smell the special fragrance he or she has. (pause) Assume that you have been with this person for a long time, that you know each other very well. (pause) Imagine meeting the person at the beginning of a date; you can feel your heart beat wildly in your chest, and you can hardly breathe. (pause) Visualize going to your favorite place for a date with this special person. (pause) Feel the good time you are having. (pause) It nears the time to go and you get into the car to leave the favorite place, (pause) You decide to go to a quiet spot to be alone, a place you love to be, where you can talk. (pause) As the person touches your hand and holds it after you arrive at the quiet place, imagine the special touch of the person's hands. (pause) Feel the excitement as you snuggle closely to this person, feeling his or her body close to yours. (pause) You have never been happier it seems; enjoy this. (pause) Feel the gentle warm breath tingle on your ear as the person whispers, "I love you." (pause) You could almost melt and you respond as you would like to. (pause) Then the voice that you have learned to love and hear so clearly says to you, surprisingly perhaps, "Let's make love" and makes a gentle attempt to undress you. This is the first chance you have had to enforce the decision you have made regarding the degree of physical intimacy and sexual behavior (since the unit on sex education).

Based on this decision, continue the scenario. If you say no, then imagine being able to say no without offending the person and then enjoying the degree of physical closeness with which you are comfortable. The evening continues to be a wonderful evening. If you say yes, then you should also complete the scenario. You have a wonderful evening. (pause) Imagine the ending of the evening as you want it to end. (pause) Imagine now the next morning and sense how you feel about the night before. If you feel good, the decision was a good one for you. (pause) Fantasize now one year into the future, and you have stayed with that person. (pause) Look at your life-style with that person; are you happy? (pause) Continue on for five years into the future and imagine your life with that person. (pause) Now go back to the exciting evening and imagine that was one of the last times you were with that person. (pause) Was the decision you made still a good one after one year? (pause) Imagine your life-style five years from that point; is your decision still good for you?

Discussion:

1. Did you feel that the decision was good no matter the outcome in the future?
2. Is it good for one case and not the other?
3. Is the decision you made what you would actually do?

Variations: A variety of romantic scenes could be developed.

Chapter 8

EDUCATIONAL IMAGERY FOR LIFE-STYLING AND SKILL DEVELOPMENT

DECISION MAKING

- Giving Information about the Decision
- Clarifying Values, Attitudes, and Emotions
- Looking at Alternative Solutions or Options
- Exploring the Consequences to the Alternatives
- Making and Planning to Implement the Decision
- **Implementing and Adhering to the Decision — Life-styling Imagery**

The two general functions that have been covered to this point in the book have been imagery to supplement cognitive learning and imagery to facilitate the steps in the decision-making process. The focus of this chapter is on using imagery for behavioral change or modification. The assumption when using the behavioral function of imagery is that the student is already knowledgeable about the skills that he/she is attempting to acquire, that decisions have been made, and that it was not a difficult decision. It is something that the student is attempting to change in his/her life-style or a skill that he/she is trying to develop. There will be two general functions of behavioral imagery strategies discussed, namely, psychomotor imagery and life-styling imagery.

PSYCHOMOTOR IMAGERY

When a psychomotor skill is to be learned or rehearsed, there is sufficient evidence, as mentioned in Chapter 2, to support the premise that mental rehearsal will help to refine the psychomotor skill. In an educational sense, when equipment is used for skill development, shortages sometimes cause students to have to wait in lines to perform a skill, causing lulls and inactivity. Psychomotor imagery can be used in the classroom for those who are waiting and will make the actual practice time more efficacious. It can also be used when no equipment is available or for homework rehearsals.

Psychomotor imagery is actually a type of simulation imagery in that a situational scenario is created for both functions. What distinguishes the function of psychomotor imagery from simulation imagery is that where simulation imagery projects the students into a decision-making scenario, psychomotor imagery projects the students into a skill practice scenario. The psychomotor skill is usually teacher directed to assure that the skill is rehearsed correctly. If the students are confident in their understanding of how to perform a skill correctly, then the strategies may be student directed with teacher evaluation occurring during the follow-up discussion.

Any educational topic that carries with it a psychomotor component is conducive to Psychomotor Imagery. Obviously, in physical education and athletics, where physical educators routinely have their students and athletes rehearse plays and movements in their minds, psychomotor imagery has a home. Dance movements and routines, blocking and tackling in football, "moves" and shooting in basketball, water skiing, snow skiing, track and field events, golf swings, swimming styles, bowling, pool, baseball batting and fielding, volleyball, field hockey, raquetball, tennis, water polo, soccer, or even hopscotch and jacks are psychomotor skills that can be improved through psychomotor imagery.

An academic area that is conducive to imagery is first aid. The fine psychomotor movements involved in cardiopulmonary resuscitation, artificial respiration, performing the abdominal thrust for airway obstruction, splinting, bandaging, patient transporting, auto extrication, bleeding control, snakebite treatment, and dealing with a wide variety of specific injuries must be refined through psychomotor imagery because of the infrequent use of first aid skills by the average first aider. Most students are not going to treat for snakebite or perform CPR very often, if ever, but in their minds they should perform the skills repeatedly to maintain their skills in case the need to perform the skills ever arises.

In the arts and crafts, psychomotor imagery rehearsal can improve skills and help the artist or craftsman to envision unique creations. As the potter imagines shaping a bowl or pot, he/she can visualize how the fingers must react to the clay to form various shapes. The artist, to paint a part of the whole canvas, must see the whole picture in his/her mind to present proper perspective and colors. The wood craftsman can visualize the shape that will be produced as he/she imagines using a router, a band saw, or as several pieces of wood come together for a useful item. The music teacher should encourage psychomotor imagery as students learn to play their instruments. As the students picture a note on a scale, they should be able to imagine depressing valves on a trumpet, positioning the slide on a trombone, pressing the strings on a violin, and pressing the valves on the woodwinds. When singing and learning to sight read, the students should practice imagining a series of notes and hear in their minds a note (if they have perfect pitch) or at least hear the relative pitches between several notes.

The chemistry teacher can promote lab safety by having the students imagine the skills in lighting a Bunsen burner, when using a pipette to transfer dangerous chemicals, or when mixing chemicals in a beaker. The home economics teacher can promote safety by using psychomotor imagery to improve sewing, cooking, and ironing skills. The auto mechanics teacher should have the students rehearse in their minds the skills involved when using the power equipment in the shop. Educational Imagery Strategy 26 is an example of psychomotor imagery (*see* Appendix).

LIFE-STYLING IMAGERY

A popular concept in health education is called life-styling or life-style analysis which in theory promotes the incorporation of healthy behaviors into the life-style of individuals. Life-styling imagery facilitates this process in several ways and functions. As with psychomotor imagery, the focus is not to have the students make good decisions but use the decision that has been made. The students are knowledgeable about the behavior, and it becomes a matter of changing their life-styles. Life-styling imagery cuts across many content areas, but an example of where life-styling imagery is extremely helpful is in controlling the amount of stress (distress) in one's life. For example, as one of many functions in stress management, life-styling imagery can help control polyphasic thinking (trying to concentrate on one thing but other thoughts keep jumping into the mind), a symptom of Type A behavior, as in Educational Imagery Strategy 27. (*see* Appendix) Other specific functions of life-styling imagery that will be discussed are role assumption imagery, habit breaking/forming imagery, and recreational imagery.

Role assumption imagery is not entitled role-playing imagery because even though role-playing is a viable teaching method, through imagery, the role that is portrayed should actually be assumed by the student. One purpose of role assumption imagery is for the student to assume the role of the ideal image of him/herself. The student's ideal image of him/herself is one that will remain constant in a general sense, that is basically a constant position on a conservative or liberal continuum in relation to values and behaviors, but the ideal image is created specific to different instructional topics. In other words, the ideal image has different perspectives as it relates to social behaviors, spiritual living, emotional wellness, fitness levels, or other dimensions of living.

The old addage you are what you think you are underlies the function of role assumption imagery. For example, if the student lacks self-confidence, then his/her ideal image, a role he or she will assume first in fantasy, is a self-confident image and he/she will portray the attributes of the self-confident individual. Through continued rehearsal and study of the image the student works to convince him/herself how that image is part of him/herself and eventually assumes the role. The role rehearsals should be in a variety of situations where self-confidence is required, such as making constructive comments in class or peer situations. Role assumption imagery is initiated in the classroom, but the role image should be rehearsed repeatedly to be in the mind of the student, particularly when situations are faced that are conducive to the ideal role. Educational Imagery Strategy 28 is an example of role assumption imagery (*see* Appendix).

Role assumption can be used for overcoming phobias or natural anxieties as well. If a person is overly anxious before making a class presentation, then *not* imagining the presentation as something that people are going to criticize or the teacher is going to evaluate is important. Instead, the image that should be developed is one that everyone is eager to hear what the student has to say since the presentation is something of value. The student assumes the role of a distinguished speaker.

Role assumption imagery can also function like role-playing or role reversals but in an imagery format. Assuming the role of parents to see the reasoning behind parental decision, becoming a dating partner to evaluate courtesies or communication, becoming a teacher for empathy with discipline, and assuming the role of a peer if one tends to ridicule are examples of role reversals.

The second function of life-styling imagery is habit forming/breaking imagery. A basic principle and practice in psychotherapy when helping clients to break bad habits is to associate mentally, a noxious image with the habit that one is trying to break. Conversely, in the positive sense, if a person is trying to form some positive habits, then pleasant, rewarding images should be associated with the desired habit.

Most students have habits they would like to break, which may be as mild as biting fingernails or cracking knuckles to more serious habits such as excessive drinking of alcohol or smoking cigarettes. The process of habit breaking imagery is to clearly imagine the behavior that the student is trying to break in a typical situation in which the behavior is enacted, and then associate it with a very noxious image. For example, if the habit to be broken is snacking on candy bars, then the teacher could direct the students to imagine a place where they purchase candy bars, such as a vending machine or a store, visualize buying the candy bar, and then the teacher could have the students prepare to eat the candy bar. Before they eat it, they should imagine the candy bar being dropped in the sewer, rubbed in the garbage, or have someone throw up on the candy bar. The next phase would be to have the student actually eat the candy bar, focusing on the vile smells of the noxious element of the candy bar, imagining how revolting the candy bar is to them. The final stage is to continue to rehearse the scenario each time candy is thought of. This will usually reduce noticeably the number of candy bars consumed. Educational Imagery Strategy 29 is an example of habit breaking imagery (*see* Appendix).

Another approach to breaking bad habits is to imagine the action of the bad habit as clearly as possible and perhaps to an extreme. If cracking knuckles is to be avoided, then when the knuckles are cracked, imagine that the inside of the finger joints are grinding against each other, that bone chips fly off as the bones bang against each other. Imagine the cracking sound from inside the finger, amplified to a deafening thunder and crackle. Even more graphic could be the visualization of blood as a part of the cracking mechanism. The scene may be slowed down so it is drawn out and brutal. This exaggerated torture to the knuckles is one example of a negative image associated with the cracking of knuckles. Another example might be when trying to control the amount of loud music to which one listens. One can imagine the sound waves crashing into the eardrum and shaking it violently, the ear ossicles rattling and crackling, and finally burning out (with sparks flying) from the electrical system (nerves). Educational Imagery Strategy 30 is a more realistic example of habit breaking imagery visualizing the action of smoking (*see* Appendix).

On the other hand, some people would like to develop some habits but because of laziness or lack of vision never get into the habit. Some people would like to keep up on current events by reading a news magazine or the newspaper, but when it comes down to it, they usually end up reading the comics and sports page with a quick scan of the front page to see if anything major is happening. Other students may want to develop habits of regular study, giving compliments, practicing relaxation skills, planning daily activities, setting priorities, visiting aging loved ones, or getting regular exercise. The positive image that can be formed by the student is something associated with the behavior, either real or or imaginary. The young man who wants to embark on a fitness program may either create a realistic future image of his body as a perfectly functioning machine, with big arteries, an efficient pump, and solid muscles, or he may see a fantasy picture such as girls flocking around him in his physically fit state. The same young man may need an image while the fitness is going on in addition to the end product image. The young man may want to develop a whole scenario with different muscle groups and organs of the body, envisioning the tear down of the muscles one day, and feeling them building back stronger the following day. The student who is desirous of reading current events may want to picture her/himself discussing the issues intelligently with peers or teachers as a result of reading news publications. Educational Imagery Strategy 31 is an example of habit forming imagery (*see* Appendix).

Recreational imagery can be used for a number of purposes including preventing boredom, escaping pressure and overload, stress management, and just for the fun of it. Where many people seek a wide variety of drugs to take "trips" or escapes, recreational imagery can produce good trips and escapes without the side effects of drugs. The only limitation to an otherwise wild, crazy, vivid, colorful trip is the individual's imagination. The student can go as far as his/her imagination will allow. Educational Imagery Strategy 32 is an example of recreational imagery (*see* Appendix).

Recreational imagery is a very valuable skill to develop when practicing the management of stressors. When a person becomes stressed when having to wait in lines, the person can escape to a South Sea island. When caught in a traffic jam, rather than churning inside, a person can be fishing alone on a mountain lake. When homework is stacking up, rather than worrying about it during lunch, breaks, or when not able to get to it, the student can escape for a few minutes and sit in front of a fireplace with someone special. Educational Imagery Strategy 33 is an example of using recreational imagery for an escape (*see* Appendix).

Chapter 9 focuses on educational imagery strategies and considerations for elementary students.

Appendix

EDUCATIONAL IMAGERY STRATEGIES

Educational Imagery Strategy 26
CPR SKILLS

Purpose: To provide students with an opportunity to practice mentally cardiopulmonary resuscitation skills.

Type: Directive; psychomotor

Monologue: Visualize yourself sitting on a park bench. (pause) Look around and see a lawn and trees that characterize the park you are in. (pause) As you are sitting there you see an older man, who is caucasion and has silver hair, in his late fifties, who is jogging. Watch him jog through the park. (pause) Suddenly you see him grab at his chest as if in pain. (pause) You see him stop, then collapse. (pause) Run over to him. His face has a bluish color to it. (pause) Imagine yourself shaking his shoulders, trying to get a response, but there is none. (pause) You then tilt his head back and check for breathing. (pause) You wish that you would feel a breath on your ear or hear some breathing, but there is none. (pause) Visualize yourself pinching off the nose, supporting the head, and putting four quick breaths into the man's mouth. Imagine the feel, the sweaty neck, the feel of pinching the nose, and the feel of putting your mouth to his. (pause) As you check for breathing again, you feel for a pulse at the carotid artery; you feel nothing. You double check, hunting for a pulse; there is none. (pause) You know that you must continue doing CPR. (pause) Imagine yourself locating the xyphoid process and placing your hand correctly on the sternum. (pause) Position your body so that you are ready to do the compressions. (pause) As you begin, imagine the feel of compressing the man's chest; you compress almost 2 inches at the rate of eighty compressions per minute. (pause) Repeating this, pushing straight down, releasing but continuing contact with the chest; you do this fifteen times. Visualize and feel this process, doing it correctly in your mind. (pause − 15 seconds) Check the pulse and breathing. (pause) There is none, so continue CPR. (pause) A friend of yours walks by − give him instructions to call for help. (pause) Continue CPR. (pause) Help arrives, and you continue CPR until the paramedics assume control of the situation. (pause)

Discussion:

1. How did you feel with the sensory component of the scenario?
2. How was your positioning, hand positions, breaths, etc.?
3. Do you think you could actually perform in a real situation as you did in this scenario?
4. How often do you think you should rehearse this kind of scenario to be ready if an emergency did occur?

Variations: The students could be left to do as they wished in a nondirective scenario after they saw the victim collapse. The teacher could then check their sequences after the scenario and then rehearse it again correctly if performed incorrectly.

Educational Imagery Strategy 27
THOUGHT STOPPING

Purpose: To help the students to develop the skill of thought stopping, a stress management strategy.

Type: Directive; life-styling

Monologue: Reflect on three classes where you have homework assignments or tests to take. Think clearly about what you have to do for the first class; (pause) remember the assignment and think what tasks it will take to complete it. I will refer to that as Class 1 study. Spend a moment now to remember the assignment of study for a second class. (Think as clearly as you can about what is involved in that study situation.) (pause) I will refer to that as Class 2 study, and finally I would like you to concentrate on a third class assignment, thinking what will be involved with the third type of study. (pause) I will refer to that activity as Class 3 study. In the next few moments, I am going to have you jump thoughts back and forth. This will take some concentration, but I want you to focus on the thoughts that I ask you to think on. I want to have you, in your minds, do a project.

I will call this activity "project" so that when I say "project" you will perform the task that I ask you to do. The project is to subtract from the number 999 the number 7 and then continue to subtract sevens until you reach 299. During the project I'll have you switch back and forth between Class 1 study, Class 2 study, and Class 3 study, and when I say "project" then you will continue with the mental subtracting. Begin the project. (pause) Think Class 1 study. (pause) Project. (pause) Class 2 study. (pause) Project. (pause) Class 3 study. (pause) Project. (pause) Class 1 study. (pause) Project. (pause) Class 2 study. (pause) Project. (pause) Class 3 study. (pause) Project. (pause) STOP. You cannot get the

project accomplished by thinking of the other assignments — concentrate only on the project.
(pause)

Discussion:

1. How many of you have experienced thinking like
   this, trying to do one project when other thoughts
   keep entering in?
2. After the stop command were you able to do better on the project than when I had you jumping
   back and forth between thoughts?
3. Could you use the same technique when you are
   experiencing polyphasic thinking?

Variations: Thinking of girl friends and boyfriends when reliving
an embarassing event, or catastrophizing (making a
minor problem major) when doing a project would
add another dimension to thought stopping.

Educational Imagery Strategy 28
BECOMING

Purpose: To help the student assume a desirable role, in this case being friendly and pleasant.

Type: Nondirective; role assumption

Monologue: Assume that you have decided that an attribute or image that you would like to project to others is that you are a friendly, pleasant person. Identify in your mind now a person of your same sex whom you think is friendly and pleasant. (pause) Visualize this person, either real or imaginary, as clearly as you can. (pause) Visualize his or her smile, eyes, and countenance. (pause) Imagine that person in a social situation, such as in a hallway or locker area greeting friends between classes. (pause) Visualize the person eating at a cafeteria or another eating place with friends, noticing very carefully the habits he or she has. Imagine what the person might be saying. (pause) Imagine now that you have those same traits. (pause) Look at yourself in the same locker area or hallway between classes, doing the same kinds of things that your friendly, pleasant person did. (pause) Imagine yourself in a similar eating situation and acting similarly to the friendly, pleasant person, except this time it is you. (pause)

Discussion:

1. How hard was it for you to imagine someone being pleasant and friendly?
2. List the traits on the board that were identified.
3. Were you able to put yourself into the role of being friendly and pleasant?
4. How many of you changed some things in your basic nature?
5. Can you become your image of friendly and pleasant?

Variations: The traits of pleasant and friendly can be replaced by honesty, integrity, enthusiastic, etc.

Educational Imagery Strategy 29

BREAKING THE SODA POP HABIT

Purpose: To have the student break the bad habit (if inter-preted as such) of drinking too much soda pop.

Type: Directive; habit breaking

Monologue: Imagine yourself going to a vending machine or a store and buying a can of pop, the kind of pop you really like but are trying to cut down on. (pause) Imagine as clearly as possible the can; feel how cold it feels in your hand; look at the color and the writing on the can. (pause) As you get ready to take a drink of the pop, a dirty, grimy person comes and spits chewing tobacco juice into the top of the drink. (pause) He spits in it again, and it makes you feel queasy. You set the can down on a radiator heater and it heats up. The drink smells like tobacco juice; it is warm and vile. (pause) Imagine now that you have to drink the pop; it is warm, it tastes aw-ful, and you almost have to gag it down your throat. You probably feel sick.

Discussion:

1. If you were to associate this scene each time you took a drink of pop, do you think you would be able to cut down on drinking it?
2. Is there another type of scene that would be more effective?

Variations: Any number of habits could be the focus of the habit breaking, and the noxious association could be sewer, or vomit.

Educational Imagery Strategy 30
CANCER STICKS

Purpose: To have students focus on what may be happening inside the respiratory system during smoking.

Type: Directive; habit breaking

Monologue: I want you to be able to visualize smoke going into your lungs. Assume that on an experimental basis you elected to take one draw on a cigarette. There is a machine that is hooked up to your chest; it looks like an x-ray machine, but instead it projects a magnified picture of your respiratory system on a large screen. Visualize taking a large puff on the cigarette and holding it in. (pause) On the screen you can see the smoke rush down the trachea; the smoke appears dark gray on the screen; you can see the cilia in the trachea get covered with smoke, and their movements slow down. Imagine the smoke pouring further down the lung. You can see little black spots being deposited along the side of the brachioles; you know that it is tar. As the smoke arrives at the alveoli, the screen magnifies the smoke and analyzes it. On the side of the screen you see a list of different poisons within the smoke. (pause) Examine the oxygen exchange. You can see at the pulmonary capillaries the carbon dioxide coming off the red blood cells, and instead of oxygen grabbing onto the sites on the red blood cells, the carbon monoxide poison attaches. (pause) Imagine now expelling the smoke, leaving behind some greyish color.

Discussion:
1. Can you imagine how emphysema or cancer could come about when the smoke irritates the lining?
2. If you were to think of this scenario each time you smoked do you think you would be inclined to smoke?

Variation: Envisioning the emphysema or cancer development process on the lungs would also be beneficial.

Educational Imagery Strategy 31

MENTAL HEALTH DAY

Purpose: As a part of a stress management unit, students should be able, as a result of the strategy, to establish the ingredients for a mental health day.

Type: Nondirective; habit forming

Monologue: In your minds, I want you to imagine three things that you like to do. Begin with the first thing and imagine doing it, in a place that you like to do it and with whom you like to do it. It should not be school or work related but something you enjoy. The activity should cost little or no money and be something you can do near or at your home. Imagine doing the activity. (pause) Change your focus now to another thing that you like to do with the same conditions as the previous activity. Think about it, do it, imagine the colors, the activity, the sounds and the people with whom you like to do it. Do the activity as soon as you identify something for this second activity. (pause)

Repeat the exercise for a third activity, but this time it must be something different than the first two but with the same conditions. Enjoy the third activity as soon as you think of one. (pause)

Now reflect on a day of the week that you could do these activities and not be bothered by work or school, for at least part of a day. Imagine doing the activities on this day. (pause)

Discussion:

1. How often do you do the activities that you imaginted?
2. Let's brainstorm on some of the activities that were done. (voluntarily)
3. Could you incorporate the activities as part of a mental health day to reduce stress levels?

Variations: Other conditions could be placed on the activity such as being a family day, something that can be done in less than a couple of hours, or it could be opened up to cost more and take longer depending on the populations and purpose of the activity.

Educational Imagery Strategy 32
THE DRUG-FREE MIND TRIP

Purpose: To allow the students an opportunity to take a trip through mind imagery, which demonstrates to them that they do not need to use drugs for mind trips.

Type: Nondirective; recreational

Monologue: Assume that you have taken a drug, something like LSD, that will give you a psychedelic trip. We are going to imagine some wild things, so let your fantasies run freely. I will give you some initial guidance, and then I want you to imagine some wild things. Visualize that you are flying through a long, colorful tunnel with the bright colors varying and mixing. Visualize the bright yellows, reds, blues, and other colors. (pause) They are circling around the tunnel through which you are flying. (pause) Imagine as you are flying through the tunnel a large ball of red is coming at you. (pause) *Hear* the color; what kind of sound is the red ball making? (pause) Imagine breaking through the red ball, and the impact splatters the colors onto the walls of the tunnel. (pause) Imagine flying out of the end of the tunnel into the clear blue sky. Fly down to a town below. Look at the streets – they are cobblestone. (pause) There are old wagons there, (pause) and people are wearing clothes from another century. Look at the women wearing black dresses with white aprons and white bonnets. They are carrying bread and fruit in baskets. There are shops along the side of the street. (pause) Snap your fingers and time stands still. Everyone freezes and does not move. (pause) Go up to the people; touch them; (pause) they feel cold. (pause) Ice begins to form on them. (pause) It builds up on them so there is an inch of ice all over them; (pause) the streets – the whole place turns into an ice age – it turns perfectly white. (pause) Suddenly

a giant monster that looks like a firebreathing drag-
on pops his head above the horizon. (pause) He sees
you and breathes fire and begins to walk toward
you. (pause) Visualize it breathing fire and melting
ice where it breathes. As he breathes on the frozen
people they melt into bright green pools of liquid.
(pause) It gets closer and closer to you. Imagine the
fire coming from its mouth and landing at your feet.
(pause) Feel the heat. (pause) You see now there is
nothing but fire around. Look at the fire on all sides
of you. See the reds and oranges, yellows, some
streaking blue. Turn around fast, like an ice skater.
(pause) The spinning makes a huge wind, and you
cause a tornado. (pause) The tornado gets larger . . . .
Complete the scenario and any other wild situations
you can think of. (pause)

Discussion:

1. How do you think the scenarios you saw here
   could be like an LSD trip?
2. How did it feel to be able to have the control to
   to get out anytime you wanted?
3. Do you really need drugs to "space out" and hal-
   lucinate?

Variations: More frightening things could produce a "bad trip."

Educational Imagery Strategy 33
ESCAPE

Purpose: To allow the students to escape mentally for a few minutes, in the process teaching them a skill they can use to combat boredom and stress from waiting in lines, in traffic jams, etc.

Type: Directive; recreational

Monologue: I want to take you on a little trip, so in your relaxed state I want you to imagine that you are going to travel very fast, flying like Superman to a beach area where you would like to go. Visualize yourself traveling through the air, flying over the ocean. (pause) Look to the distance and see the beautiful beach area that you would like to visit. (pause) Imagine arriving and landing on the beach; you are no longer Superman but just yourself; you are wearing what you would like to wear. (pause) Look around and see the white sand. (pause) It is warm but not hot. (pause) The water is clear and beautiful. (pause) The waves are just the size you hoped they would be. (pause) Look at the trees, some palm and other kinds; see them rustling with the gentle breeze. (pause) The temperature is perfect for you. (pause) You may want to be alone, or there may be other people. (pause) I want you to smell the sea breeze and other smells associated with this beautiful scene. (pause) Imagine walking along the beach — feel the wet sand under your feet (pause) and the wave covering the tops of your feet, and you stroll barefoot along the shore. (pause) You have all the things that you want provided. If you want to lie in a hammock between two trees, you need only to visualize it. If you would like company, you only need to provide it. You will have all the skills you want. If you want to surf, you will be able to do it; if you want to just lie down and sunbathe on the sand, the conditions will be perfect. Enjoy your stay for the next few minutes.

Discussion:

1. Was the experience enjoyable?
2. Are there times when a scene like this might help you to wait in a line, tolerate a traffic jam, or overcome boredom?

Variations: The scenes that may be described may range from any peaceful scene in front of a fireplace in the mountains, perhaps with a winter scene, a mountain scene, or any other variety of settings.

Chapter 9

EDUCATIONAL IMAGERY
WITH ELEMENTARY SCHOOL STUDENTS

Although there are some special considerations when using imagery in the elementary classroom, the main purpose of having a special chapter to deal with imagery in the early years is because educational imagery is more effective with young children than with adults in most cases. The principle reason is that imagery or make-believe is a natural part of childhood; although fantasy is natural with older students, the younger children are uninhibited about sharing fantasies, and it is, in fact, part of group and individual play. Cowboys and Indians, Pirates, Cops and Robbers, Dress up, House, Army, Tarzan, Superman and Superwoman, and Wonder Woman all flow naturally from the minds of young students. Imaginary ropes, guns, bows and arrows, horses, and food often evolve from simple wooden sticks, blocks, or nothing at all. If there is no one to play with, children solve the problem by creating pets, enemies, friends, and relatives and even introduce the imaginary friends to their parents.

This healthy power of imagination can be channeled much easier than with older students or adults, even though the potentials are the same. Somewhere in adulthood, much of that creativity and free imagination is lost unless it is nurtured. Unlike older students, children do not need to close their eyes, tune-out everyone else in the class, or dim the lights. They have shown that they can produce clear images on command, which allows the teacher to use special environmental adaptations and preparations. This is not to say that students of this age group do not respond well when put into educational imagery strategies similar to those described in other chapters in this book; in fact, they generally respond better than adults, as long as the strategies are short.

SPECIAL CONSIDERATIONS

Outside of the natural considerations that an elementary teacher gives students in elementary school, such as selecting topics that are appropriate for the age group, using terminology and concepts that children can understand, and avoiding major moral-behavioral conflicts, there are a few special considerations when using educational imagery with the early elementary student.

1. *Dealing with Values:* With older students, the process of values clarification is often used because adolescents are in the process of forming their own value systems. Younger elementary children are still relying heavily on parental/religious values to guide them until they are able to formulate their own values. The consideration is that instead of leading the students to open-ended value decisions as the teacher does with older students, the students are encouraged to be directed to more obvious, socially accepted values in a directive sense. Values such as honesty, not taking what is not yours, the Golden Rule, and other noncontroversial values should be used and heavy moral issues avoided.

2. *Screening for Disadvantaged Children:* The elementary school is where there often exist many undiagnosed mental and social problems with children. When children enter school for the first time, they have been through five or six developmental years using parental models that are either good or unfortunately not as good. Neglected, abused, and unloved children find themselves with problems that many children do not experience. The teacher then needs to be sensitive to the variety of students and their needs. The teacher, before using an educational imagery strategy, should reflect upon the possible types of images that the students may be seeing as a result of the teacher-directed scenarios, remembering that a positive image to one may be a negative image to another.

3. *Length of the Scenario* As mentioned previously, the length of the educational imagery strategy must be shorter than the attention span of the students. In early elementary school, the

strategies become shorter because of the shortened attention spans. The exception to this is when the imagery strategies are active make-believe imagery; then the length can be increased.

4. *Decision Making:* In this book a great deal of emphasis has been placed on the decision-making process and using imagery to foster that process. Making decisions of a complex nature may not be suitable for children, who may not be able to make good decisions because of limited experiences. It is recommended that scenarios not leave the student in a complex situation such as those described in Chapter 6 on Simulation Imagery until they have the maturity to deal with and cope with the decisions. It is good to have the students make simple decisions and progress to the more difficult decisions which improve their decision-making capabilities. Generally speaking, educational imagery strategies are better for elementary students if they are teacher directed. Educational Imagery Strategies 34, 35, and 36 are examples of elementary school oriented methods (*see* Appendix).

ACTIVE IMAGERY

Active imagery is really what children call make-believe. Channeling the fun of make-believe to accomplish educational objectives is the best way to define active imagery. There are three main differences between active imagery and the other functions of imagery described in this book. First, instead of having children lying on the floor, motionless, with their eyes closed, the students are moving and active. Second, the students interact with each other, and the teacher supplies constant feedback during the strategy. Third, the students are supplied with props, pictures, and other stimuli to enforce the educational quality of the experience. Elementary teachers now use make-believe effectively making indepth descriptions unnecessary here. Educational Imagery Strategy 37 is an example of active imagery (*see* Appendix).

The next chapter will give several examples of educational imagery strategies.

Appendix

EDUCATIONAL IMAGERY STRATEGIES

Educational Imagery Strategy 34
WATER CYCLES

Purpose: To understand and enforce the cognitive concept of where rain comes from (having already described the water cycle). (geared toward elementary school students)

Type: Directive; cognitive reinforcing

Monologue: Imagine that you are a drop of water among millions of drops of water on a lake. Imagine floating on the surface of the water. See how blue and clean the water is. (pause) It is a warm day, and you can look up and see the sun. (pause) It feels so warm on you — enjoy how relaxed you feel — floating among the other drops of water. (pause) Feel yourself getting hotter and hotter until finally you feel yourself turning to steam. Imagine yourself as a drop of water becoming very light, and you rise above the the water. Feel yourself rising, floating, high in the sky. (pause) Look down and see the lake far below with trees around it. (pause) You begin to cool off now, since you are so high — it seems fun. (pause) Look around and see other little clouds of steam like yourself, and you decide to get together with them. Imagine forming a big cloud with all the other puffs of steam. See yourself as part of the big white cloud. (pause) It begins to get very cold, and as you get colder, part of you begins to turn back to water. (pause) You feel yourself getting heavy, as if you may drop any moment. (pause) As you look around, your other friends in the cloud are having the same problem, and your cloud is turning dark. (pause) You see many of your friends turn to drops and begin to fall. (pause) You try to stay up but finally you give up — you turn to water and you start to fall. (pause) Imagine falling, which seems like forever. Imagine the thrill. (pause) Finally you see the ground coming very fast and splat! You land, but it didn't hurt. (pause) You see that the ground is wet from all the other raindrops that fell before you, so since there is no room to seep into the soil you and several other drops start floating along the surface of the ground. (pause) You find others and you form a little creek. (pause) Imagine the thrill of tumbling over the rocks and around corners as you flow down the hill. (pause) Ahead you see a lake and you rush right into it. Imagine again floating along the surface enjoying the bright sun.

Discussion:

1. How many of you have seen steam?
2. Did you know that was water?
3. Did you ever think that a cloud might be like steam?
4. What other forms does water come in?
5. What is snow, sleet, hail?
6. Why can't you see steam off a lake when it is hot but you can when it is cold?

Variations: The water droplet could go into the earth and go through a plant and evaporate on the top of a leaf.

Educational Imagery Strategy 35
LIKE POPEYE'S SPINACH

Purpose: To help students to eat their vegetables.

Type: Directive; habit forming imagery (geared toward elementary school students)

Monologue: Imagine that you are eating dinner at home. As you sit down,your favorite main dish is on the table, and you can visualize someone putting a helping on your plate; you can hardly wait to eat it. (pause) You see that there is something to drink, but all of a sudden you see the vegetable. It is your least favorite vegetable, and a serving is on your plate. Imagine look- at your plate; imagine the smell of your favorite main dish (pause) and also the vegetable. (pause) Imagine first that you are going to eat the vegetable to get it over with so you can eat the main dish. (pause) As you begin to eat, you think it will taste bad, but as you take a bite, you don't think about the taste. (pause) You know it has lots of vitamins and minerals and you forget about the taste and instead feel the strength and energy it gives you. (pause) Pretend that the vegetable is like Popeye's spinach and you suddenly become strong. (pause) Imagine making your chest larger (pause) and your arms stronger, (pause) and you attack that vegetable and gobble it up. (pause) Finish the rest of the meal and imagine how good it tastes.

Discussion:

1. Every time you eat a vegetable, do you think it would be easier to eat if you were to imagine getting instant strength from the vegetable?
2. Do you think you can remember to do this each time that you eat your vegetables?

Variations: Students can actually imagine being Popeye, Wonder Woman, or another hero who eats vegetables.

Educational Imagery Strategy 36

GERM SPRAY

Purpose: To encourage children to protect others from their disease-carrying spray from sneezing and coughing by covering their mouths. (geared toward elementary school students)

Type: Directive; cognitive reinforcing

Monologue: Imagine that you feel as if you are going to sneeze; (pause) you can feel your nose itch, your nostrils flex, the skin on your nose and cheeks begin to quiver. (pause) As if you had no choice, you take a big gasp of air, filling your lungs. (pause) As you exhale, you let it go and force the air out as a relieving blow; it feels good and cleansing. Focus now on the air that has left your mouth and nose. Imagine magnifying the spray several times, and you can see the droplets of water among the air that is being expelled. The water droplets are saliva, some carrying germs. Imagine the spray in slow motion going out 6 or 7 feet and landing on someone else, germs and all. (pause) Repeat the slow motion sneeze, spraying still another person with your germs. (pause)

Now imagine that you are walking by someone else who has to sneeze. You can see that the person is going to sneeze. (pause) He/she is looking at you. (pause) He/she gasps the air, but the sneeze comes so fast that it doesn't let you get out of the way. (pause) See the expelled air and water droplets come your way — imagine them coming at you and land on you.

Discussion:
1. How can you avoid spraying and getting sprayed?
2. Can you see how disease sometimes spreads?
3. How important is it to be aware of this?

Variations: Coughing, focusing on the bug, etc.

Educational Imagery Strategy 37

MAKE BELIEVE DOCTOR

Purpose: To help students learn about their bodies, learn about the career of a physician, and overcome fears of going to the doctor.

Type: Directive; active

Props: Tongue depressors, thermometers, mock physical forms (writing or pictures for those who cannot read)

Monologue: We would like each of you to pair up with a classmate, and we want to have you make believe that you are a doctor. We want you to pretend that you are already grown up and that you really are a doctor. We will help you to do the things a doctor does. The person who is not the doctor the first time will get to be the second time, but for now we want you to pretend that you are really going to see a doctor. All of you should imagine that we are in a doctor's office and that we are not at school; pretend the other students are also patients and doctors.

The patient will first come in and ask for a checkup. (pause) Doctor, talk to the patient as you will. Ask the patient to breath deeply, and listen to the breathing through the stethoscope on his or her back. Move the stethoscope around. Have the person continue to breathe deeply. (pause) Listen now for the heartbeat on the chest (note that older elementary students may need to be paired with the same sex). Feel the pulse now on the wrist; (pause) count the number of beats in a minute. (pause) Take the patient's temperature for two minutes. (pause) Open the mouth with the tongue depressor and see the uvula and see if the throat is reddened. Look at the eyes; as we dim and brighten the lights, notice how the pupil expands and contracts. (pause) Check the knee reflex by gently doing a "karate chop" directly

under the kneecap. (pause) Check off on the physical form the things that worked well. (pause) Say
goodbye to the patient. (pause) Now change roles
and the patient becomes the doctor.

Discussion:

1. Questions related to the different bodily functions, i.e. why do eyes dilate and contract, why
   the knee jumps, etc.
2. What do you think a doctor is doing when you go
   see him? Why does he do the things he does?
3. Is there a reason to be afraid of doctors?
4. What are some good things about being a doctor
   when you grow up?

Variations: Students can make believe without stethoscopes, or
they could even be more elaborate using otoscopes
and ophthalmoscopes to look at the retina of the
eye and the ears, although some cautions are obvious. Other professions could also be explored,
e.g. police, business, aviation, etc.

Chapter 10

ADDITIONAL EDUCATIONAL IMAGERY STRATEGIES

Educational Imagery Strategy 38

CELL WARS

Purpose: To reinforce cognitively the functions of antibodies in the body for warding off infection. (geared to younger students)

Type: Directive; cognitive reinforcement

Monologue: We are going to imagine a battle between two forces, the red intruders and the white defenders. The city that the invaders attack is a white city, with white buildings, white stores, and the soldiers wear white uniforms and helmets. The city will be one in the future such as a city during the "Star Wars" era. Visualize as clearly in your mind as you can the futuristic city, all in white, and it all appears to be made of plastic. Imagine soldiers walking around in their white uniforms. (pause) Notice that they all are carrying large rifle like weapons over their shoulders. Around their waists are white gun belts. In the belts are harpoon bullets, 5 inches long, which dangle from the belt. Each bullet is a different shape, and they look somewhat like an assortment of keys. The people are walking on a white walkway that is bordered on the left by a tall white wall. Suddenly a red intruder appears on the wall. He looks like a

134

red Darth Vader type, and he is carrying a laser gun. As he stands up on top of the wall and readies his laser gun, you notice that right in the middle of his chest is a uniquely shaped hole that looks like a keyhole. (pause) Suddenly the red invader begins to open fire on the city. (pause) The laser strikes the buildings and tears large holes in them. (pause) Visualize the white soldiers grabbing their rifles and loading the key like bullets into the rifle ends. They begin to fire back at the red invader. The first bullet hits the invader right in the hole of his chest but is bounced off in a trail of sparks. The key bullet did not fit the hole. The red invader laughs loudly and zaps more structures with his laser. (pause) A whole series of bullets comes from the white soldiers, but they again bounce off the red invader. Visualize the laser flashing and the white soldiers bombarding the red invader with the shower of bullets. (pause) Finally a bullet from one of the white soldiers hits the red invader right in the middle of the hole and the shape of the bullet fits exactly. It plugs the hole and the invader topples backward off the wall down to the ground. Imagine the soldiers returning to their patrolling duties. (pause) Soon, another red invader creeps up on the wall. He has a hole in his chest that resembles a star but is uniquely shaped. The invader raises his laser and again the battle begins. The white soldiers begin to fire at the red invader, who attempts to destroy the city with his laser. The white soldiers continue hitting the red invader in a blaze of sparks, but none of their bullets seem to fit the star like hole in his chest. (pause) The soldiers keep trying. Suddenly the red invader splits in two and there are two red invaders. (pause) Visualize them splitting again into four, and again into eight. (pause) Imagine the battle. (pause) During the battle, a soldier in the background is looking at the chests of the invaders through binoculars and is sketching the star-shaped hole onto paper. Imagine him running the paper to a building. In the building there are shelves and shelves of bullets, but no star bullets. (pause) The white uniformed plant operator looks at the sketch and brings out a star-shaped mold and begins to make the star bullets. They come out perfectly, and he is very pleased. He makes more and more, and the plant workers begin to load them into a jeep like vehicle. Return to the battle and now there are many red invaders, and the city is being destroyed. The white soldiers are unable to neutralize any of the enemy. Suddenly from the rear of the battle comes the jeep that is loaded with the star bullets. The white soldiers rush to the jeep and begin loading their guns. The soldiers are careful to hit their mark. The first star bullet hits dead center in the chest of one of the red invaders and fills the hole and immobilizes him. Complete the battle scene with the white soldiers neutralizing the rest of the red invaders with the bullets. (pause) Following the neutralizing of the red invaders, imagine the work crews beginning to rebuild the city and the soldiers returning to their patrol.

Discussion:

1. How does this war scene relate to the antigen-antibody wars in our body?
2. Why do the keys have to fit the hole of the invaders to be similar to the antigen-antibody comlex in the body?
3. What would happen if our body did not produce the right bullets or antibodies? What would eventually happen?
4. How often do you think these kinds of wars take place in our body?

Variations: A war depicting phagocytosis would also be interesting. Scenes could be cops and robbers, cowboys and Indians, or a game such as football. "Star Wars" background music during the war scenes would add effect.

Educational Imagery Strategy 39
ANGEL DUST

Purpose: To inform the students about the consequences of taking angel dust and facilitate their decision about using the drug.

Type: Directive; consequence imagery

Monologue: A choice you can make is to take phencyclidine, so let's explore the consequences of taking the drug. Assume that you have made the decision to use phencyclidine in the form of "angle dust." Assume that you have inhaled the drug and are now going to experience the effects. (pause) Imagine yourself standing but not feeling like you are standing. (pause) Sense that you have no idea where your feet are. Try to walk in your mind, not knowing where your feet are or having control over them. (pause) Imagine yourself as being an empty nobody, being small, not human, just a block of something in a great big laboratory. (pause) Imagine that you feel entrapped in your clothes. (pause) Take the view now of watching yourself "freak out" — tearing off some of your clothes while walking down a street. (pause) Imagine yelling, (pause) breathing hard, (pause) sweating, (pause) See that you have taken off all your clothes and are running uncontrollably down the street. (pause) Imagine yourself vomiting, (pause) Look at the people around you; you see friends looking at you during your uncontrolled time. It only makes you dizzy; (feel the dizzy feeling) during these moments you twitch and fling your arms. You see yourself, naked, still in the street, sitting next to a telephone pole; you have vomit all over your naked body, you smell, you are breathing hard, people are looking at you. See the police pick you up and you struggle and they throw you in the back of the car. Imagine trying to talk to them, but you make little sense — you have trouble

controlling your tongue and your speech is inco-
herent. (pause) Return your focus to the classroom.

Discussion:

1. How realistic is the picture that has been painted?
2. Was it difficult for you to imagine yourself doing that?
3. What are your attitudes about angel dust?

Variations: A variety of other drugs could be used except the scenario would need to be changed according to their actual effect.

Educational Imagery Strategy 40
INSTANT AGING

Purpose: To help students avoid stereotyping older people to promote more youth and older person interactions.

Type: Nondirective; role assumption (key discussion question has life-styling implications)

Monologue: I would like you to look to the future. Imagine yourself graduating from high school (if high school students or younger). Imagine wearing the cap and gown; picture going through the line with other students and getting your diploma; imagine who will be there to give you a hug upon completion of the ceremonies. (pause) Imagine now that you are going to do your life's work. Imagine selecting an occupation, or if you decide to be a homemaker then imagine the training to become the best at what you decide to become. If you need to go to a university, then imagine the university experience. If you are going to develop a trade, then picture the trade school, etc. (pause) Imagine selecting a partner who is your dream man or woman. See the courtship, (pause) the romance, the emotions. (pause) Imagine that you make a commitment to him/her, by marriage or other arrangement that you choose. Visualize your professional or homemaking skills and you become what you want to become in your midyears. (pause) Imagine that you are successful. (pause) Imagine the ideal life-style. Time passes and imagine that you are approaching old age. You have had children perhaps; picture those children, if you have any. (pause) Imagine the life-style that you would ideally have in retirement. Imagine where you would want to live. (pause) Visualize the activities that you would like to do. (pause) Imagine your family visiting you. (pause) Think of the good life you are having. (pause) Imagine that you lose your partner; you are sad, but you adjust and imagine how you can still be happy. (pause) Spend some time in this scenario. (pause)

Discussion:

1. How many of you had good older lives?
2. Were you in a rest home or your own home?
3. What are some of the things that you did?
4. How many of you had families around you?

Key Question: What are you doing now to help someone you care about who is older to enjoy the same kind of life that you envisioned for yourself in old age?

Variations: A negative old age could be envisioned.

Educational Imagery Strategy 41
PRO-LIFE

Purpose: To share the perspective of the right to life groups related to abortion.

Type: Directive; emotional

Monologue: I want you to imagine that you are going to go into the uterus of a pregnant female. Visualize as clearly as you can that you are in a large, pear-shaped cave, which is the human uterus. The walls are bright red with rich, nutritive blood. At the large end of the pear-shaped cavity you see some openings you know are the fallopian tubes that lead to the ovaries. (pause) As you look up at one of the openings at the top of the uterus, you see an egg drifting into the uterine chamber. (pause) Look at it clearly, and you see the miracle of cells dividing into more and more cells. (pause) Visualize the path of the egg as it curves and nestles into the uterine wall across from you. (pause) It lodges there and continues to divide. You notice that the blood vessels begin to form and the placenta develops. (pause) Over time you see that the little ball of cells begins to take some shape and you can recognize a head, (pause) a spine, and then you can see the limbs begin to form. (pause) It has been several weeks as you have been watching the growing and now you can see that there is some activity going on in the little human form. (pause) You can see the heart begin to beat. Visualize the little red heart beating very fast, like a bird. You can see the eyes and little webbed fingers on the hands. (pause) The little fetus is still enclosed in a sac, but it is clear and you can see the development. (pause) You can see some movement in the fetus as you know that nerve and muscle development is taking place. You see that the fetus is now sucking the thumb. (pause) The embryo is now over an inch long, with webbed hands and feet, and the sex organs are almost distinguishable — it appears that it will be a little boy. (pause) Observe this miracle of creation. (pause)

Suddenly, you see entering the lower part of the uterus (the small end of the pear) a long, narrow, silver instrument with a hole in the end. See it probe around and locate the embryo. See suddenly the instrument start suction and begin to take in fluid. As the end of the instrument approaches the embryo you see the sac tear from the protective wall of the uterus and be drawn toward the suction instrument. The protective amniotic sac is suctioned into the instrument and gone. Now the embryo that you have been watching gets suctioned into the instrument, tearing the embryo into parts. The heart stops, it is no more. The instrument continues to vacuum the uterus.

Discussion:

1. How serious is this event?
2. What are the good reasons for making it happen?
3. Was this a life or only potential life?

Variations: Other abortion techniques could be imagined, such as saline injection or D and C.

Note: The discussion questions must be handled carefully; students should not be forced to respond to this. *This is a biased strategy.* It may be that the teacher may want to follow this strategy with a pro-abortion perspective to maintain balance.

Educational Imagery Strategy 42
TRADITIONAL VERSUS LABOYER

Purpose: To have the students mentally experience childbirth once in a traditional birth and once in a modified Laboyer delivery. (Note: This is a pro-Laboyer strategy.)

Type: Directive, emotional

Monologue: Try to imagine yourself as a baby in your mother's womb, just getting ready to be born. (pause) As you look around you see that you are covered by a membrane and that you are in a fluid environment. (pause) Occasionally you feel the red lining of the uterus contract and force you down into the birth canal; it is hard because you are cramped already. You can feel the pressure on your head as the uterus continues to contract. You feel the membrane break as you feel the fluid run to the outside of the birth canal. Sense the feeling of manipulation as you continue to be pushed out. It is dark, you are warm and feel close to the environment as you hear the mother's stomach sounds and are constantly nourished by her. You feel frightened now because you hear your mother screaming occasionally every time you feel the contractions. (pause) Things are changing rapidly — you feel the exit. Soon your head is out. You cannot even open your eyes because the bright lights are blinding; you try to open them because you know you are leaving your mother, but your eyes have never seen bright lights before. (pause) As you are delivered, you miss the touch of your mother. With your eyes still closed, you hear the person who has grabbed you say, which seems so loud, "It's a boy" or "It's a girl." It frightens you. (pause) It is so cold compared to where you were. (pause) You have an incredible urge to breathe for the first time, but as you open your mouth to breathe, the air burns your lungs. It is so traumatic, you hesitate to breathe. Suddenly, you feel someone snapping your foot. It hurts; (pause) with the bright lights, the loving mother contact missing, the noise, having to breathe, and now getting hit, you just have to cry and cry you do. The nourishing embilical cord which is still pulsating and supplying you, is suddenly cut off – you are on your own. You feel someone shoving a rubber point up your nose and in your mouth and sucking out the fluids. You feel yourself being passed on to another person, who takes a piece of cloth that feels so rough and starts wiping you; you wonder what happened to the peaceful fluid environment. You feel yourself being placed in a bed with glass walls; you are alone. They put a heater over you and it feels better. You sense that the adjustment to the new world is going to be rough. (Note: After discussion of the Laboyer delivery repeat the scenario as follows:)

Imagine now that you are again going to be delivered; visualize yourself in your mother's womb; feel the contractions again as you begin to be forced down the birth canal. The embryonic sac again breaks. There are no screams to frighten you because your mother is breathing through the contractions; you still sense that something strange is going on, but you have no reason to fear yet; it is quite painful squeezing down the canal though. As your head is delivered, there are hushed whispers; you sense there are others around, and because the lights are dimmed you can open your eyes and see. As you breathe, you let out a little cry because it burns, but you are placed on your mother right away and her touch is reassuring, so you stop crying. Her gentle caress feels good. (pause) You can feel the life-supporting cord begin to stop feeding you but the security of your mother's breasts is helping the transition. (pause) You have a feeling of getting nourishment from your mother. When the cord quits pulsating, they cut the cord, but you do not notice it.

As you snuggle next to your mother you can look around; it is blurry but you can see for the first time. (pause) The room is warm and the same temperature as the womb that you left. The father picks you up, which frightens you for a moment, until you realize that he is putting you in a warm water bath. It feels like the womb, and you can now stretch and move about. (pause) You look up and see your father smiling as he gently strokes you and washes you off. When he is through, he places you in a blanket, which is rough, but you are placed again with your mother, who nestles you.

Discussion:

1. What do you actually think goes through the mind of a baby when delivered?
2. Do you think the Laboyer advocates have a point?
3. What potential wrong is there in doing a Laboyer delivery?
4. What were you able to visualize and not able to visualize?

Variations: Some postdelivery scenarios could focus in on the issues of nursery versus mother care, with emphasis on the mother fatigue and need for rest versus the loving care the mother can give.

Educational Imagery Strategy 43

THE TOTAL PERSON

Purpose: To have the students focus on their multiple dimensions of being and contemplate how they can assume idealization or self-actualization in each of the five dimensions. Upon completion, the students should visualize assuming the role of their actualized total person.

Type: Nondirective; role assumption

Monologue: I want you to focus on your dimensions of being, that is, the different parts of your life that make you unique. We are going to have you focus on your social self, physical self, intellectural self, spiritual self, and emotional self. I will let you focus on each of the dimensions, and most of the imagination will be left to you. First focus on your social sense, becoming self-actualized in the social sense; imagine several scenarios where you assume optimal social behavior. Change the focus now and concentrate on your physical state. Visualize your optimal state as you would like your realistic state of physical wellness. Imagine situations that will help you become that physical ideal. (pause) Change your focus now to your intellectual self and imagine a realistic ideal and becoming self-actualized in your intellectual sense. Picture how you will accomplish your potential in your intellectual sense. (pause) Identify some situations in which you will be able to see your optimal intellectual state, such as taking a test or discussing issues in class. (pause) The spiritual dimension should now become the center of your focus of attention. Imagine your ideal spiritual state. Imagine some scenarios that have you demonstrating that optimal state of spiritual health. (pause) Focus now on your emotional state. Think of some situations where you will optimally cope with anger and fear and demonstrate love and other complex emotions in an actualized state. (pause)

Discussion:

1. Were there any dimensions for which you could not imagine an ideal?
2. Was there a scenario in which you had obtained the ideal?
3. Is working for these ideals worthwhile?

Variations: Giving a situation for each dimention would be more directive and allow the students to respond in an ideal sense to each of the situations based on their image of self-actualization.

Educational Imagery Strategy 44
DRINKING AND DRIVING*

Purpose: To provide a situation in which a student will have to make a choice about drinking and also whether to ride home with someone who is drunk.

Type: Nondirective; simulation

Monologue: Think of a person with whom you would like to go to a special event; someone of the same sex, a friend. This friend may be close or not, and he or she may drink socially at a party; you may not be sure. This person must be able to drive and have access to a car (parents', friend's car, etc.) Can everyone imagine that person?

Visualize the detail of the friend you have just identified; be sure you see him or her clearly; see the person's smile, notice the color of the hair and what the person would be wearing if he or she were going to a social event with friends. (pause) Imagine yourself with your friend on the doorstep or entrance to a place that you might go to attend the social event or where several others will be gathered. (pause) Visualize yourself entering the place where other people are gathered and see the surroundings. See several people sitting around on the furniture. (pause) See the furniture in the room, the pictures if any, the window furnishings if any, the lights and other features in the room. (pause) See the people in the room; some you recognize and others you may not. Imagine some people who would be at that party that you know, and visualize them sitting or standing. (pause) Imagine several others that you do not recognize but you can see them. (pause) You can see in one part of the place where the event is being held that alcohol is being served. See beer, mixed drinks, and pop on a table with some crackers, pretzels, etc. (pause) Imagine that your friend

*Thanks to Raymond Johnson for this strategy.

goes off to talk to someone else. (pause) Decide whether to sit down or stand up, but get comfortable. Look around and see that most people have drinks in their hands or close by them. See one male whom you do not know who is standing up with a mixed drink in his hand and is giggling uncontrollably. (pause) See someone else whom you may have recognized sitting quietly in a corner and staring.

Imagine yourself greeting people, meeting people, and having a good time at the party. Also decide what you will drink if anything. Enjoy the party. (long pause) Imagine now that it is time to go home and you find your friend. You notice that he/she has obviously been drinking to the point that coordination is impaired. Imagine leaving the party and going out to the car that your friend has driven. (pause) Arriving at the car you have a decision to make about saying something about his/her ability to drive or remaining silent. If you stay quiet, imagine the type of ride home you will have, perhaps getting in an accident. If you say something, imagine that the friend protests and refuses to let you drive; imagine the conversation and complete the scenario and get yourself home safely.

Discussion:

1. Did you drink as much as was good for you if you did drink?
2. Were you happy with your decision?
3. What were some of the alternatives to riding home with your drunk friend?

Variations: You could continue the progressive strategy by getting in the car, driving with the friend with several near accidents, and making another decision.

Educational Imagery Strategy 45

THE JOGGING CRAZE

Purpose: To prepare students in fitness/health courses to explore the consequences of beginning or not beginning a jogging program (assuming all students can potentially jog).

Type: Directive; consequence

Monologue: Having discussed jogging as a type of exercise, I would like you to imagine beginning a jogging program. Visualize where you would like to start — a track, through your neighborhood, or somewhere else. (pause) Visualize the type of clothes you will wear to jog. Imagine wearing them, putting on your jogging shoes, and see the colors. (pause) Picture yourself doing some stretching and warm-up exercises. (pause) Now imagine yourself taking off the first time; it feels pretty good for a few hundred feet, then your muscles begin to feel a little weak. (pause) Feel yourself start to breathe heavily. (pause) You begin to perspire. (pause) You keep going and you begin to feel it hurting all over, and you feel as if you just have to drop. (pause) You stop and walk, breathing heavily. (pause) After a moment you try again, but imagine yourself again getting tired much too quickly. It is depressing.

Change the scene to getting out of bed the following morning; your muscles are sore; you can hardly move them. (pause) You feel that jogging was a mistake perhaps. The pain is terrible as you think of attempting to jog again. (pause)

Three weeks have passed and now imagine the scene before, starting to jog. (pause) After hard weeks of jogging regularly, you are wearing the same clothes, and you begin your jog. (pause) This time you look around at the scenery — focus on the jogging area you have selected. (pause) Imagine that you are breathing hard, but it doesn't bother you a

great deal — you keep going. Complete the scenario
of how long you think you will want to jog after
three weeks. Imagine completing the distance and
stopping to walk. (pause) You feel tired and are
sweating, but you feel refreshed. (pause) Imagine
the good it is doing your body, the strength that
you feel. Your step is livelier, and you feel good
about yourself. You find that you are maintaining
or approaching your ideal weight. (pause) Imagine
yourself fifteen years in the future, still jogging. Picture how you will look.

Change the scene now and imagine your life-style
without jogging. (pause) Imagine getting tired easily
when walking up stairs, (pause) when trying to play
games at a park. (pause) Imagine fifteen years ahead,
without jogging or any exercise, how much weight
you have gained.

Discussion:

1. Do you think the agony is worth the good feeling
   at the end of jogging?
2. If you choose to begin a jogging program, is the
   means to attain fitness clear to you?
3. If you choose not to jog, is there another form of
   exercise you want to do, or did you become
   sedentary?

Variations: The poor model of the nonjogger could have been
more directive, with weight gain, muscle weakness,
muscle tone, and other factors added to the descriptive nature of the scenario.

Educational Imagery Strategy 46

THE TRYOUT

Purpose: To help students, particularly those beginning a new school (such as entering high school freshmen) to evaluate rationally the outcomes of trying out for athletic teams, drill teams, cheerleading teams, bands, choirs, etc. The choices examined here are to try out or not to try out.

Type: Non-directive; consequence imagery

Monologue: I would like you first to identify an extracurricular team or group such as an athletic team, drill team, band, debate team, choir, or other group to which you may like to belong. (pause) Imagine now that you are going to audition for that group. To do so, I want you to visualize as clearly as you can the surroundings of the tryout situation (an athletic field, a gymnasium, a choir room, band room, etc.) Imagine the equipment and materials that will be associated with the tryout, the smells of the room, the other students trying out, the sounds of the situation. (pause) Imagine the degree of nervousness you feel as you practice and perform. (pause) Imagine your audition, whether it is one-day tryout or something that takes several weeks. (pause) Imagine now that you have been successful in becoming a member of the group. Complete a scenario that has you enjoying membership in the group. (pause)

Change the scene now to completing the audition and looking on a bulletin board and not reading your name, or listening for your name to be called out and it is not. (pause) Complete the scenario of how you will feel, (pause) how you will tell your friends or guardians, and perhaps the excuses you will make. (pause)

Change the scene again, and imagine now that you did not try out. Focus on the feelings you might have, the questions you have as to whether you could have made it or not. (pause) Imagine your school life-style without trying out for any group. (pause) Imagine the stress you avoid by not trying out. (pause)

Discussion:

1. Were you able to imagine making the teams and was it gratifying?
2. Were you embarrassed or did you feel bad when you were not chosen? Did anyone have a particularly bad experience whey they did not make the team?
3. Which is a worse situation — having tried unsuccessfully to make a team or not trying and never knowing how you would have done?

Variations: Include more focus on the nature of excuses, i. e. not making the team, only talking of trying out without following through, etc.

Educational Imagery Strategy 47

STAGES OF DYING

Purpose: To help the student recognize the stages of dying based on comments the identified loved one makes. Skills should be developed that facilitate talking to a dying loved one, depending on the stage of dying.

Note: This strategy is too long for most populations. The teacher should use perhaps two or three of the five stages described here.

Type: Nondirective; cognitive reinforcing and emotional

Monologue: Picture in your mind a person now living that you love very much — a parent, a girl friend/boyfriend, a spiritual mentor, or some other loved one. Visualize the detail of the person's face, eyes, hair, mouth. (pause) Feel as you touch his or her hand, shoulder and perhaps cheek. (pause) Smell the fragrance the person eminates. (pause) See his or her smile.

Change the scene to being called to answer a phone call. (pause) The voice on the other end is that of an acquaintance both you and the loved one have in common. The voice states, referring to the loved one you just envisioned, that the person has been diagnosed as having a rare disease and will not live longer than a couple of weeks. Feel your emotions. (pause) Hang up the phone and proceed to travel to the hospital where the loved one will be. (pause)

Picture now a hospital room, a private room in the hospital where your loved one will be. (pause) Visualize the window, (pause) the curtains that provide privacy for the patients. (pause) See the white linens (pause) and the sterile equipment of the room. (pause) Smell the smell that only a hospital room has. (pause) You see the flowers and plants on a small table — the cards have your loved one's name on them. (pause) The curtains are screening the loved one so you do not see the person but you know he or she is there. Feel your heart beat as you worry about what you will say. (pause)

Call the person's name softly. (pause) He or she responds with a "Hi, please open the curtain and visit." See yourself opening the curtain. (pause) There you see your loved one, with a smile. (pause) You ask the question that you have asked so many times before, but now with great meaning as you reach for the person's hand, "How are you?" He or she responds weakly, "I'm fine. This is only a little setback — I am going to beat this thing. I heard they are doing some research on this right now and some people have been cured — I'll make it." Reflecting on this stage of dying, respond as you would respond. (pause) Continue the conversation. (long pause) Say goodbye and leave the room.

You decide to return to the person, times passes, a whole day. (pause) Imagine yourself now entering the room — (pause) a nurse is leaving and whispers to you, "He/She had a rough and painful night." (pause) You see the person again in the bed, (pause) the smile is gone. (pause) Again the question you ask, "How are you?" The response is, "Why me, I can't believe there is any justice in the world. It just is not fair." Give your response. (pause) Continue the conversation. (long pause) When you are through, leave the room and proceed home. (pause)

Time has passed, a couple of days. (pause) Again you can visualize yourself going into the now familiar room (pause) See it and smell it again. (pause) You see the loved one with eyes closed and you gently call the person's name. The loved one opens his or her eyes and a weak smile comes to the face. "How are you today?" you ask. The response you can hear is, "I have been praying." This might be a surprise to you if the person is not religious, but if he or she is, you expect it. "I have pledged to God that if I can live a few more years I will live a life that He would be proud of." Respond as you would. (pause) Carry on a conversation and leave when you are ready.

Imagine a day passing. (pause) See yourself entering the room. (pause) The loved one is lying in bed, staring at the ceiling. (pause) He or she doesn't notice you enter. Picture the person. (pause) You see a tear drop down the side of his or head. You call the person's name, but instead of a response, he or she glances your way, then stares at the ceiling again. (pause) You ask, "How are you?" The loved one shakes his or her head, obviously very sad and depressed. Respond to the person. (pause) Imagine yourself leaving the room.

Time passes and this final time you enter the room and you see that the person has grown weak. As you enter, see the person smile at you and motion you to come in. The loved one looks very weak but has a twinkle in his/her eye. (pause) Before you can speak the loved one says, "I have been waiting for your visit; I want to tell you how much I love you. I am going to die, but it's okay . . . ." Carry on the conversation.

Come back to the classroom.

Discussion:

1. Were you able to visualize all the visits?
2. Could you see your loved one?
3. Were you comfortable talking to the person?
4. Let's list some of the things you were able to say during each of the visits.
5. Do you think that if a tragedy were to occur as we described here you would be able to visit the person?
6. Could you or did you fluctuate with the person's stage?

Variations: Select two or three stages of dying rather than all five. The student could go through the stages of mourning.

Educational Imagery Strategy 48

WHO'S WHO IN THE EMERGENCY ROOM*
(Allied Health Career Education)

Purpose: To help students in a health career education course facilitate the development of attitudes toward openness to review work as part of quality assurance, behaving ethically and sympathetically when responding to patient needs, and appreciation of the seriousness of potential harm to patients and the necessity for maximal accuracy.

Type: Nondirective; values clarification/simulation

Monologue: Imagine yourself arriving at the hospital where you work as a phlebotomist (technician who draws blood). You are perhaps a little nervous, as it is your first week on the job. As you enter the laboratory you begin thinking about your new supervisor. Dur- the past week you have developed a feeling of confidence in your supervisor. She has assisted you with a few difficult venipunctures and offered you helpful suggestions for obtaining difficult specimens. She has, however, been demanding of the phlebotomy staff. She expects specimens to be collected promptly and strictly according to procedure. On last evening's shift, you remember seeing her scold one of your former classmates for collecting a blood gas specimen incorrectly.

As you approach the laboratory blood drawing station, you meet your supervisor. She greets you and begins explaining your assignment for this evening's shift. One of your co-workers has called in sick and the work load is excessively heavy. Your assignment is to cover the Emergency Room and laboratory while she and another cover the floors. As she hurries off, you ponder the situation. Although you are a little uncertain as to your ability

*Appreciation to Dean Sheehy for developing this strategy.

to cover the assignment, you are determined to do your best. As the evening progresses, you manage to keep pace with the blood collection requests. You are particularly pleased with the way you handled the blood collection on that scared three year old over in the ER.

The sound of sirens interrupts your thought. Two ambulances and a police car pull up next to the ER. Two severely injured patients are wheeled in. The phone rings. It's a request for you to make collections on two other patients in the ER. You hurry to make the pickup because you know you will be called again soon for requests on the newly arrived patients. You pick up the request forms at the ER desk and head to the patient area. The two patients are in adjoining rooms. You notice neither patient has been banded for identification yet, due to the crisis situation created by the arrival of the trauma patients. No one is around to ask, so you read the first slip; it reads Mr. Johnson. You ask the first patient if he is Mr. Johnson; he responds. You make the collection and follow the same routine with Mr. Jackson in the next room. You return to the lab and give the specimen to a lab tech for processing. A half hour later you return to the lab to pick up a urine specimen on Mr. Jackson. You suddenly discover that the person whom you thought was Mr. Jackson is really Mr. Johnson. The realization of what has happened runs through you. You must decide what to do. Many thoughts run through your mind: Whom should I tell? Will it really make a difference to the patient if I do tell? Will I lose my job? Now complete the scenario as you would as a phlebotomist. (long pause)

Discussion:

1. What are possible medical and emotional consequences to the patients involved if incorrect labotory data are used to evaluate their medical status?

2. What is the importance of the realistic assessment of one's own level of knowledge, understanding, and ethical responsibilities in the health care environment?
3. What approaches did you use if you discuss the situation with the supervisor?

Variations: Use a moral dilemma for a nurse, physician, radiologic technologist, or other health care provider.

Educational Imagery Strategy 49
THE CAFETERIA*

Purpose: To have students evaluate their food choices.

Type: Nondirective; simulation

Monologue: Assume that you've been studying all day for a really difficult test tomorrow, and you stop for a moment for a break. You are hungry. Your stomach aches slightly as you think of the last time that you ate, which seems like forever. You decide to go to the cafeteria (maybe it's your dorm cafeteria, a smorgasborg, or school cafeteria where you have many choices). As you walk in you smell the aroma of good, warm food. (pause) The longer you wait in line, the hungrier you become, but luckily the line is rather short. (pause) As you approach your turn in line you can see several of the colorful foods displayed on the serving table, and again you begin to think about what you would like to eat tonight. (pause) You pick up a tray and the silverware, which feels warm from recently being washed, and place them on your tray. (pause) You slide your tray a little way down so that you can see all of the salads at once. (pause) Look at all of those salads. The jello salads, the macaroni and the potato salads, the vegetable ones, the tossed green, and there are always your favorites, which are usually hard to resist. (pause) Let's see, which one? Or should you eat two or three? (pause) You carefully make your selection(s) and watch the lady put the salad(s) in the dishes and hand them to you, or you may decide not to have any. Now, you move on to the meats. You feel the warmth from the warming lights and moisture from the steam rising from the various meats. (pause) Smell the warm food. (pause) There are so many to choose from; you notice they even

---

*Appreciation to Nancy Young for developing this strategy.

have turkey, roast beef, ham, and fish. You take a minute to think about this and make a choice, (pause) or decide not to have any meat. You approach the vegetables. They look really fresh. Notice their crisp color — the greens, the yellows. Decide which, if any vegetables you will choose. You make up your mind, realizing that there are several people behind you and that you are slowing up the line looking at all of this food. (pause) You see the breads (rolls, biscuits, cornbread, buns). (pause) You decide whether or not to have one to enjoy with your meal. (pause) You place this on your tray and spot the desserts. (pause) Look at all the pies. (pause) They even have the kind of cake you like and also fresh pudding. (pause) You decide on one or more desserts or decide not to have a dessert. (pause) You reach for ice tea, water, coffee, or milk. (pause) Finally you reach the end of the line and your bill is added up for your choices. You pick up your tray and begin to consider where to sit. (pause) Imagine choosing a place against the wall. You walk over (pause) and then you unload your food and place the tray on another empty table beside you. (pause) Enjoy eating the food. (pause) Feel how good it feels as it fills your stomach. Feel how warm it feels to your body. (pause) You are full and feel relaxed. (pause) It feels good just to sit for a minute and feel relaxed and full. (pause)

Discussion:

1. How many food groups did you fill?
2. How many calories did you get?
3. How important was taste in your decision?
4. How important was nutritive value?
5. Did you overeat?

Variations: Shopping for a meal at a grocery store or eating with friends who were buying junk food would vary the scene.

Educational Imagery

Educational Imagery Strategy 50
I DO

Purpose: To have students view marriage from two perspectives, from their own idealistic perspective and then from the perspective of potential partners. To create an awareness of how adjustments will need to happen in preparation for marriage.

Type: Nondirective; values clarification/simulation imagery

Monologue: Each of you take a moment and imagine as clearly as you can the ideal marriage situation for you. (pause) Imagine each of the situations as clearly as you can with the spouse you select. In addition to imagining who your spouse might be, imagine the situation in your home. Who will do what chores, who will do the budgeting, (pause) shopping for groceries, (pause) who will take out the trash, (pause) garden work, (pause) lawn care, (pause) auto maintenance. (pause) Which spouse will work, or both. (pause) How many children, (pause) what kinds of names you like for children. (pause) Will you give your child spankings and/or other types of physical punishment; (pause) hours you like to sleep (pause); how much time you want to spend with the in-laws. (pause) Do you imagine relocating from your hometown. (pause) Do you want children right away; (pause) What kind of child delivery do you like to do? What kinds of pets do you want? Who does the cooking? Imagine more of the ideal lifestyle.

During the break here, the class will have a discussion with both male and female responses listed on the board.

Now imagine the same marriage situation except with a different perspective. Imagine changing your situation to conform to perspective as listed by the opposite sex. Complete the scenario.

Discussion:

1. How difficult was it for you to make alterations in your ideal marriage scenario?
2. Do you think you would have to make as many adjustments if you were really to get married?
3. How hard do you have to work at a marriage to make it work?

Variations: Having students do just the opposite for each of their choices would eliminate the class discussion, which in some cases would be beneficial.

Educational Imagery Strategy 51
TO PULL OR NOT TO PULL

Purpose: To help students reflect on the emotional issues associated with euthanasia.

Type: Nondirective; emotional/consequence imagery

Note: This strategy should not be used if anyone in the class has recently experienced a traumatic death in the family.

Monologue: Picture in your minds a parent or guardian who has just experienced a severe accident. The prognosis is not good; the person is in a coma and not expected to come out of it. If the person does come out of it he or she will likely be a "vegetable" because of the extensive brain damage. The person is being kept alive by life-support systems. Imagine that person you have identified in a hospital room on a bed as though asleep. (pause) Look carefully at the person's features, the hospital gown. (pause) The person looks a little thinner than you recall. (pause) The person is hooked up to tubes going into the arms, which supply nourishment. (pause) Another machine is on the side of the bed with a mask over the person's face, providing oxygen. (pause) Another machine is hooked to the chest to maintain the hearbeat. (pause) Smell the smells of the hospital room and look around at the sterile environment. (pause) You are faced with a critical decision as the doctor and other family members enter the room and talk to you. Picture the doctor. (pause) Picture others involved in the decision. (Pause) He says, "You may want to seek a court order to have us remove the life-support systems, because the liklihood of your parent or guardian coming out of the coma is not very good, and the problems he/she will have if he/she comes out of this are tremendous. We can keep him/her on life support for a long time but it is very expensive; what will you have us do?" Complete scenarios, one when you remove the life-support systems and one when you keep the person on the systems. Consider the emotional, financial, spiritual, social, and other aspects of the decision. Complete the scenarios; ultimately you must cast your vote on what action you will recommend to other family members.

Discussion:

1. Did you consider what others thought?
2. Did you consider what the person in the coma might want?
3. There is not a positive outcome in either of these two scenarios but one you may have to experience; could you make a decision?

Variations: To make the strategy less emotionally draining, the student could be briefed on an older person, a child, a drunk, a minister, and a variety of other people and make the decision for the doctors to remove the life-support based on sketchy biographies.

Educational Imagery Strategy 52

STRESS MANAGEMENT

Purpose: Having completed a unit on stress management that includes the understanding of the nature of psychosomatic phenomena, physiological responses to stress, instrumentation to identify stressors in one's life, with practice of stress management strategies, the students will identify two stressors that they will modify, change, or control and practice implementing those strategies through the imagery strategy prior to implementing them behaviorally.

Type: Nondirective, simulation

Note: This strategy will have to be exceptionally vague because of the diversity of stressors and controlling strategies the students will identify. Generally speaking, the students will be visualizing themselves practicing progressive or autogenic relaxation, meditation, biofeedback, charting biological rhythms, meditation, altered states of consciousness, saying no, or a variety of social and personality engineering strategies. This strategy should occur after the student has had practice with several strategies, since much of this is up to the student to create.

Monologue: Think about the first stressor that you have chosen to eliminate or control. (pause) Feel the emotions involved when that stressor works on you. (pause) Sense the determiniation you have to eliminate that stressor. (pause) Relax (autogenic by now), take a few deep breaths. (pause) Imagine yourself in a situation where the stressor will potentially affect you. Sense all of your surroundings — the smell, (pause) the noise, (pause) the colors. (pause) Now, imagine yourself in a relaxed and calm fashion, eliminating or controlling the stressor in the manner you anticipate doing it. (long pause) Feel how good it feels to have controlled it; sense how your body is relaxed and functioning well because you have mastered it.

Think now about the second stressor that you have chosen to eliminate or control (repeat the monologue of the first stressor).

Discussion:

1. How many were able to visualize the stressor situation?
2. Was it hard to overcome the stressor?
3. Do you think you can overcome the stressor when the situation actually arises?

Variations: This strategy could be more directive, having the students practice specific stress management strategies.

Educational Imagery Strategy 53
SAYING NO

Purpose: To allow the student an opportunity to rehearse mentally how to say no to a friend and still maintain the friendship without succumbing to peer pressure.

Type: Directive, life-styling

Monologue: Reflect back to the last time that you felt overloaded, when you had just too much to do or at least all you could handle; perhaps it was homework, a project, studying for an exam. (pause) Take a moment to remember how stressed you felt, how every minute seemed to be full, how you wished you could just make it through the "push" to get things done. (pause) As you relive this overloaded time, imagine yourself doing what was overloading you. (pause) Imagine that you are being productive in accomplishing what you needed to do, feeling that if you continue to be this productive, you will make it through the crisis. (pause) Imagine now a friend with whom you like to do things. (pause) Imagine the details of the friend, what he or she might be wearing, what kind of mood he or she might be in, and the person's physical features. (pause) Reflect on an activity that you and your friend like to do together. (pause) Imagine the scenario that has you doing what it is that is making you stressed, and imagine that friend approaching you and asking if you would like to do the activity that you and your friend like to do together. Imagine clearly the friend making the offer. (pause) Complete the scenario with you saying no in a way that does not offend. (pause) Imagine the friend putting on some pressure for you to forget your project and imagine again how you will be able to stay with your project so you will be free of the stressor.

(pause) Imagine completing the task that was stressing you — imagine doing the activity with your friend without the burden of the task on your shoulders.

Discussion:

1. How many of you actually would have said no to your friend?
2. Was it difficult to say no?

Variations: This could have been a nondirective simulation activity in which the student was given the choice to say no or not, followed by the feelings associated with procrastinating.

Educational Imagery Strategy 54
THE DRAMATIC ENDING

Purpose: To allow students to clarify their values regarding funerals and to promote an atmosphere of acceptance that people to fantasize about death.

Type: Nondirective; affective values clarifying

Monologue: I want you to fantasize today about your own death, I don't want you to think about the pain or any ugly type of death, in fact it should be a heroic death or a dramatic death, a way that you would like to die if you had to. For example, perhaps if you could imagine carrying the football over for a touchdown after a heroic run in the big game as you pass over the goal you die, people run out and cry over you, or perhaps a dramatic death would be to collapse by your locker when everyone is passing by between classes. Take a moment now and imagine your dramatic or heroic death.

Complete the scenario now by imagining your funeral with all the details. Will you be buried before a memorial service? Will you have an open casket funeral? Will you be cremated? What clothes will you be buried or burned in? What will your casket or urn look like? Who will attend the funeral? How will they respond? What will they say? Complete the scenario of your own funeral to the point of putting your remains to rest.

Discussion:

1. Would anyone like to share the way he or she died?
2. Was it difficult to imagine how you might die?
3. How often do you think that people think about death in this way?
4. What were the things that were important to you at the funeral?
5. What was important to you in your dramatic death, to have people there or not?

6. Was it important to have a fancy funeral or was a simple one acceptable?
7. Did you want your family and friends to be happy or sad?
8. How sacred is the body after you die?
9. Did any of you give your body to science? Donate organs?

Variations: The strategy could be more directive and lead students through a fancy, rich type of funeral, a simple one, and then a cremation type of funeral, and then discuss the result with which they were most comfortable.

The next chapter will present guidelines for developing Educational Imagery for the individual teacher's specific needs.

Chapter 11

TIPS FOR DEVELOPING
EDUCATIONAL IMAGERY STRATEGIES

The strategies in this book are only a sampling of the many types and topics that can be effectively presented through educational imagery. Teachers are encouraged to develop their own strategies relevant to topics they see as vital, using the functions of imagery. Experience using the strategy has led to several considerations when developing personalized educational imagery strategies.

LENGTH OF SCENARIO

It has been found that the length of the scenario depends upon the length of the attention span of the students with whom the teacher is working, which is difficult to assess due to the wide variability among students. It also depends upon the nature of the scenario. It was found that if the scenario was light, positive, uplifting, and motivating, then the students were able to go as long as fifteen or twenty minutes on the college level and twelve to fifteen minutes at the secondary and elementary school levels. If the scenario was negative, depressing, or emotionally heavy, then the scenarios could not last longer than about eight to ten minutes before some of the students experienced difficulty concentrating.

The first time it was realized that difficult scenarios should be short was with a class of 125 college personal health students. It seemed appropriate in a unit on death and dying that a good skill for the students to develop would be to be able to talk to a dying loved one who was going through a particular stage of dying or or coping with death. The purpose was for the student to select a loved one, imagine hearing the news of the terminal diagnosis, then visit the person on five different occasions. The first occasion the students imagined visiting their loved one when the patient was in the denial stage, then the anger, bargaining, depression, and last the acceptance stages. During each mental visit, the student was directed to the point of awareness of the stage through which the person was passing, and then the student was to carry on a conversation with the loved one. The first three stages seemed as though the strategy was going well, but when the students went back for the fourth time during the depression stage, some students reported that they began to break concentration, and only about 60 percent of the class was able to complete all the scenarios, which lasted twenty-five minutes. The students' feedback indicated that with "heavy" topics, a couple of short scenarios was all they could deal with effectively without becoming emotionally drained.

On the other hand, when doing recreational imagery with people going to their favorite place, doing what they wanted to do, it was found that after twenty minutes some people complained that they did not have enough time to do all that they wanted to do. Generally speaking, if the strategy is completed in fifteen minutes including the relaxation introduction, it will be very effective. When in doubt, make the strategy shorter.

A major reason that the educational imagery strategy is so valuable is because of the short amount of time it takes. Where values clarification, simulation games, and debates sometimes take the whole class period to complete or even several class periods, educational imagery is a hard hitting, practical approach that puts closure on a topic most effectively and on a very personalized basis in just a portion of the classroom hour.

UPLIFTING VERSUS DEPRESSING STRATEGIES

It is important for the teacher who uses educational imagery to remember that the strategy is very powerful potentially and that power can have a positive or negative effect. Except for instances such as consequence imagery, the imagery strategies should be a powerful positive or productive type of scenario. Students should be making the decisions they want to, becoming their ideal image of what they want to be, etc. Even in the example above of talking to a dying friend, which was a very emotional and difficult strategy, the focus was on the positive because the students were mentally preparing themselves to help the dying loved one through a crisis. They became, through their imaginations, a tower of strength to loved ones in time of need.

Negative or depressing scenarios are justified when students make choices that could potentially do harm or encourage life-style change. For example, in consequence imagery, perhaps the students could follow the choice of smoking cigarettes, and seeing themselves coughing, ill, with emphysema or cancer at a later age would be depressing but may be beneficial in making a decision. The advantage of consequence imagery is that there is a positive choice to be made that neutralizes the negative scenario.

WHEN TO USE IMAGERY

Except in the case of readiness imagery, which is used prior to presenting a cognitive concept, most educational imagery strategies are best suited after the cognitive portion of the unit is discussed. In decision-making and life-styling imagery, the strategies rely on the cognitive and affective components of the issues to help the students make wise decisions or incorporate the behavioral aspects of the topics into their lives. By ending a unit with educational imagery, the question "So what?" is answered, it puts closure to the topic and answers the question of why the topic was included in the curriculum.

During the class period itself, it is suggested that the imagery strategy be used at the end of the class, allowing just enough time for processing the strategy. Students need to be prepared for the strategy in addition to the ways mentioned in Chapter 3. The students should also have cognitive discussions about the topic, which gives the students a chance to change gears from their before-class activities. It is difficult to have students do imagery when they are "cold."

Having the strategy at the end of the class also provides a safety mechanism for the teacher. If the teacher is having the students lie on the floor to do the imagery strategy, then there is a commotion factor when the students return to their seats. It is recommended that the students, upon completion of the scenario, stay in their relaxed position while the teacher processes the experience that allows the students to stay in the position until the bell rings, ending class.

BRING THE STUDENTS BACK GENTLY

When constructing your own strategies, it is important to build in a gentle return to environmental awareness. When the students are concentrating on a particular scenario and the teacher suddenly states "Okay, that's enough!" and starts processing, it is likely that the change would be difficult to cope with and be shocking. On the other hand, a gentle return to the discussion would make the experience more pleasant. Consider the following monologue following an educational imagery strategy:

> Please complete the scenario within the next few seconds (pause). Again, concentrate on your breathing and gradually bring your awareness to the fact that you are in a classroom (pause). You should now become aware of others around you (pause). Make my voice primary in your thinking. You may open your eyes when it is comfortable (pause).

The students, following the gentle comeback, would then be ready for discussion. The gentle awakening to reality is not included in the examples of educational imagery strategies in this book, but it is assumed that something similar to the monologue above would be included.

UNIVERSAL LANGUAGE

In the actual writing and presenting of the strategies, it is important that all students be able to identify with what the instructor is describing; this not only has content implications but also wording implications. The following list of words and phrases exemplifies how the universal nature of the strategy can be attained:

Use	Don't Use	Comments
Where you sleep	Your room, your bed	Some may not have a bed or a room

Use	Don't Use	Comments
A loved one	Boyfriend, girl friend or a particular relative	Some may not have a particular relative or a girl/boyfriend
Your home	Your house	Some may not have a house but a trailer
A place you like to go for . . .	Any specified place	Some may never want to go to the identified place
Converse with a spiritual mentor (having previously defined spiritual as religious, relationship with nature, or basic morals and values)	Church, religion or form of diety	Some students are atheistic, non-Christian, and do not align with any one faith

The only time you can use specifics is when you know the background of everyone in the group or perhaps using the strategy in religious settings. It is hoped that the strategies in this book exemplify the use of this principle.

REINFORCING THE IMAGES

To assure that students are clearly imagining the scenario that the teacher is describing, it is beneficial to reinforce continually the sensory aspects of the scene. Built into the scenario should be some of the following phrases and commands to accomplish this:

Visualize the colors of . . .
Notice how large or small . . .
See the shapes of . . .
Imagine the furniture, carpet, wall decorations . . .
Imagine the sound it would make . . .

Hear the voice as he/she talks . . .
It smells so good . . .
Listen to the sounds of . . .
You recognize the smell of . . .
Imagine yourself touching the . . .
It feels as you would imagine it . . .
The soft, rough, sticky, texture feels . . .
Taste the . . .
Your mouth waters as you imagine the taste of . . .
Sense how your body feels as you . . .
Your whole body feels the emotion of . . . as you . . .

Each time the phrase is used the student should respond with an image that reinforces the scenario and thus make the strategy more efficacious.

SILENCE AND PAUSES

`To reiterate a point made earlier, the power of imagery is giving an opportunity to students to internalize the concepts presented in class. The process occurs when the students are not receiving any other sensory stimuli, including the voice of the teacher, hearing other students around them, or outside noises. The implication is that the teacher, in addition to creating an atmosphere in the classroom for mental isolation to take place, must also build in pauses of silence into the strategy. Even in directive imagery strategies, the pauses must be built in to allow the student to receive directions and form described images. One of the most difficult things for a teacher to do is to let the class be silent, because we associate silence with nonproductivity. In the case of educational imagery the silence is the most productive time.

CONTENT SELECTION

When selecting content for the development of educational imagery, the teacher should review the basic concepts of educational psychology and development. This book does not explain the concepts but reminds the teacher that different age groups cannot gain the same benefits from the same strategy. What may help an

adolescent in coping with his or her sexual development could
have very negative effects on an elementary child. This point is
fairly obvious in most cases, but some are not clear. A review of
Piaget's stages of cognitive development, Erikson's eight stages of
development, and Kohlberg's stages of moral development would
be good concepts to have in mind when developing the strategies.

DIRECTIVE VERSUS NONDIRECTIVE STRATEGIES

The natural tendency for teachers is to guide the students too
far into the imagery strategies when the students are making the
decision or doing their life-styling. The teacher should lead up to
the point where everyone in the audience would be able to identify, then let the students complete the scenario. The application
of this suggestion is more difficult than initially perceived. It
would seem easy to say about drinking alcohol, for example, that
"a friend offers you a drink at a party where most people are
drinking." Imagining that scenario may be difficult for two reasons. Some students may not have close friends who drink due to
preference, parental influence, or religious reasons, so the situation becomes unreal because the friend whom they are envisioning would never offer them a drink. The second reason is that
some students have never been to, nor would let themselves go to,
a party where drinking is going on, so the image never becomes
clear. If the instructor takes the students to the party and has the
drink offered by the friends, some students may be lost. In order
for the student to make a choice, perhaps the introduction to the
strategy should be to select an acquaintance who could potentially drink to be the person who offers. The other approach is
that if the friend they select does not drink, as far as they know,
then the phrase in the scenario directly following the offer of the
drink by the friend would be "perhaps this completely surprises
you." The second problem of the student choosing to go to a
drinking party can be remedied by describing a "social situation
such as a party" where you might attend. Then the alcohol can
come out as a surprise factor.

In the cognitive strategies, when the teacher is directive all the
way through the scenario, the instructor must be sure that the
concepts are correct and will not infringe upon individual rights of

choice. For example, if an imagery strategy were being used to reinforce a concept about blood transfusions or preventive immunizations, presume that the teacher builds the strategy focusing on the good it does. Perhaps the instructor, to show the good, would describe a scenario for the student to witness the "antigen-antibody war" with immunization and without immunization. The strategy could be very reinforcing to most students, except for those students whose religions do not endorse the medical practice of immunizations or blood transfusions. Modifications could be easily made to modify the strategy and still have an "antigen-antibody war."

VARYING STRATEGIES FOR LARGE AND SMALL GROUPS

The strategies normally will not vary if the groups are large or small, but there are some minor modifications that must be made for the large group or when the group numbers over fifty students. It is advisable not to have the students lie down with too many people unless there is a lot of space. Second, the time involved in the strategy generally becomes shorter as the group gets larger. Conversely, when groups get smaller, such as ten to twelve in a seminar format, the strategies can last much longer. In one seminar class of graduate students, the instructor used a progressive consequence imagery strategy where the students made three consecutive decisions and followed the outcomes, of which all students reported good concentration during the half an hour. It is doubtful that educational imagery could be conducted nearly that long in a large class.

In large classes, space becomes an important factor and reminders are necessary not to touch each other even if sitting very close. The instructor should emphasize the importance of mentally tuning out others in large classes. Coughing, sniffing, clearing of throats, and sneezing are all potential external stimuli that could reduce effectiveness. It is sometimes valuable to devote some time in class to practicing the tuning out of these factors. Practice is suggested by having the students concentrate on an image or on their breathing; then the teacher can introduce some external sounds and encourage the students not to focus on or hear the sounds.

BEING CREATIVE

With most teaching strategies, teachers have to look at the logical, financial, ethical, time, and other constraints to teach a concept in an ideal fashion. With educational imagery there are no limitations, and the teacher's mind must go beyond the traditional approaches to teaching. There are many approaches to enhancing the creativity, of which two will be explained here. (For more information read "Strategies for Creative Emergence" in *Health Education,* Jan./Feb., 1981, by the author) Creativity can be fostered first by taking some time and thinking of the most ideal way of teaching a concept with no restrictions. Sometimes teachers' minds have been geared toward the confines of the classroom so that they cannot think creatively this way. In other words, if you are teaching about a rare disease in the Soviet Union, then the ideal way to teach that concept is not to see a film or lecture but to take the class by plane to the Soviet Union, look at the "bug" under a microscope, catch the disease to know how it feels, cure themselves, etc. In a general sense this is ridiculous, but it is the best way to teach about the disease. Through imagery, the instructor can take that trip to the Soviet Union. Another "wild" idea for the ideal way to study the health dilemmas of an alcoholic is to take the class down to the local pub, teach them all to drink, teach them to use alcohol as a mental crutch, give them some emotional problems, build up their tolerance levels, turn them all into alcoholics, and even have them uncontrollably hurt some of their loved ones. Then the class would experience rehabilitation by taking antibuse, going through psychotherapy, attending Alcoholics Anonymous, etc. Again this is an unreal concept, but through imagery it can be done, as this type of thinking about alcoholism was used for Educational Imagery Strategy 8.

Creativity can also be fostered by using a forced matrix with the topics that should be covered in the classroom on one side of the matrix and the functions of imagery on the other side. When the function and the topic join at the intersection, then putting the topic to a particular function generally triggers a strategy in the mind of the developer. For example, the following matrix was used to develop some of the strategies in this text (Figure 11-1).

Classroom Topics \ Functions of Imagery	Cognitive Readiness	Cognitive Reinforcing	Emotional	Spiritual	Values/Morals	Simulation	Consequence	Psychomotor	Life-styling	Habit Breaking/Forming	Recreational	Role Assumption	
Mourning for the dead													
Stages of dying		47											
Aging theories													
Food quackery													
Career choices												37	
Euthanasia			51										
Overcoming fear of going to a dentist													
Abortion methods			41										
Drug trips											32		
Suicide													
Coping with overload									53				
Using "thought stopping" as stress management									27				
Finding emotional outlets			6										
Adolescent identity crisis													
Self-esteem													
Making decisions including the spiritual dimension			11										
Parenting (coping with two year old tantrums)			23			42							
Birth methods	42	42											
Safety hazards in the home													
Food choices							49						
Understanding the alcoholic			8										

Figure 11-1. Forced matrix for fostering creative educational imagery strategies.

As noted in the forced matrix, there are a number of educational imagery strategies that resulted from this method of creativity. It can be seen that for each topic there could be several strategies made merely by changing the function of the educational imagery strategy.

INSTRUCTOR SKILLS

Teachers should realize that much of the success of the strategy directly relates to their presenting skills. The instructor who gets too wordy or too descriptive and does not allow time for students to imagine the scenario will not find the strategy effective. The instructor should not hurry through the strategy or give any indication of stress in his/her voice. The voice, as mentioned earlier, should be soft, calm, and confident without stumbling over words.

It is speculated that the instructor who is not convinced that the strategy is valuable should not use this because it will be projected in the presentation. The confident, enthusiastic approach seems best and the only one used at this point. If the instructor is unsure of his/her ability to respond to students' comments and effectively guide the students, or if the teacher is worried about how the students will react, he/she will likely transmit that hesitancy to the students.

If the instructor cannot imagine the scenario she/he is describing and does not do so during the presentation of the method, it is unlikely that the strategy will be effective. However, if the instructor is excited about what the students will gain, has memorized the sequence in the scenarios, is confident in his/her abilities, has practiced a softer/smoother voice for the scenario, and enthusiastically processes the strategy afterwards, then educational imagery potentially could be the most rewarding strategy the teacher will ever implement, as has been the case with the author. More positive teacher evaluations, input from students, open discussions, and candid positive comments have occurred since using educational imagery than any other method used to this point, and the author has been enthusiastic about many other methods.

The last chapter will report the response of students who have experienced educational imagery in their classes.

Chapter 12

STUDENT REACTIONS TO EDUCATIONAL IMAGERY

The motivating factor that encouraged the author to continue in the development of educational imagery was the overwhelming positive reactions by the students. Student discussions invariably resulted in comments indicating that the students had (1) clarified their values and identified how their value came to them, (2) renewed their spiritual dimension of being and evaluated their behaviors in accordance with the spiritual roots, (3) retained images of concepts that helped them remember much longer, and (4) helped them know the logical course in making decisions and having confidence in those decisions. Their comments indicated that educational imagery made learning fun, held their interest longer, and made them feel that they themselves had the major responsibility for learning and were active in the process.

Currently there is research being conducted to give objective data as to the measurable cognitive, attitudinal, and behavioral changes that may occur with educational imagery, although these kinds of data are beyond the scope of this book. Subjective questionnaires have been given in personal health courses to students who have experienced three educational imagery strategies during the semester course. The questionnaire, which included two general questions, was given directly after each strategy. The first question was an assessment to determine the degree to which students were able to imagine the scenario and was worded as follows:

During the educational imagery strategy, I was able to (Check the appropriate response)

	Very well	Fairly well	Not at all
A. Visualize the situation and surroundings	———	———	———
B. Feel the emotions of the situation	———	———	———
C. Perform the behaviors requested	———	———	———
D. Smell the smells of the situation	———	———	———
E. Hear the sounds of the situation	———	———	———

The questionnaires were given three times with different educational imagery strategies given each time. The first time Educational Imagery Strategy 47 was given, the second time 44 was experienced, and the third time 52 was administered to the students. The results of the questionnaires are given in Figure 12-1.

Sensory Task	1st, 2nd, or 3rd Time $_b$	Very Well $_a$	Fairly Well $_a$	Not at All $_a$
Visualize the situation and surroundings	1st	51	45	3
	2nd	72	25	2
	3rd	83	15	1
Feel the emotions of the situation	1st	51	37	11
	2nd	54	36	9
	3rd	81	13	5
Perform the behaviors requested	1st	24	56	17
	2nd	57	35	7
	3rd	76	23	0
Smell the smells of the situation	1st	16	39	44
	2nd	24	33	42
	3rd	36	38	25
Hear the sounds of the situation	1st	26	47	26
	2nd	35	39	25
	3rd	39	45	15

a = the numbers in these columns represent the number of students that reported out of a total of 99 students that filled out all three questionnaires.

b = 1st, 2nd, or 3rd time means the number of times the students had experienced the Educational Imagery strategy.

Figure 12-1. Students' perceived sensory abilities during educational imagery.

The second general question that was administered to the student was worded as follows:

Place an X between the two descriptors at a position that indicates your feeling in relation to the two descriptive words. For example, if you felt that the technique was a waste of time, indicate the degree by placing an X near the "waste of time" phrase rather than the "helpful" word.

The technique was:

Very helpful__ __ __ __ __ __ __A waste of time
Boring   __ __ __ __ __ __ __Very interesting
Bad for me   __ __ __ __ __ __ __Good for me

After the experience, the students reported that on a scale of one to seven (the number of spaces placed between the words), with one representing "a waste of time" and seven representing "very helpful", the students' average mark was 5.44. When one represented "boring" and seven represented "very interesting," the average score was 5.88. When one represented "bad for me" and seven represented "good for me," the average score was 4.89.

The second time the students experienced an imagery strategy, the results were 6.03 toward "very helpful," 6.78 toward "very interesting," and 5.78 toward "good for me." The third time an educational imagery strategy was given in class, the scores were 5.98 toward "very helpful," 6.35 toward "interesting," and 6.5 toward "good for me." The following scales show the comparison of the three educational imagery strategies.

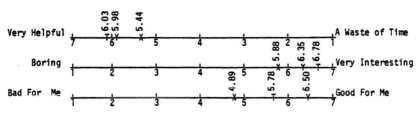

X = First Experience
T = Second Experience
Y = Third Experience

There appear to be two reasons that the students improved their scores or varied their scores from the first strategy. In the first strategy, the imagery strategy was an emotionally draining strategy and fairly long, which likely resulted in lower scores for the first time. The second reason was that it was the first time they had experienced educational imagery, and the experience was new to them. The class did not trust the strategy, had difficulty tuning out environmental distractions, and had not developed trust in the instructor, since it was early in the semester. On subsequent strategies the scores improved because the students began to enjoy and benefit from the strategies and likely made a better effort to experience the desired outcomes.

PARTING WORD

The strategies and functions contained in this book are workable, powerful strategies for the right teacher used in the proper situation. Overuse of the strategies may result in the decline in effectiveness of the strategies. Educational imagery is designed to be used only occasionally, such as the concluding method following an instructional unit. The power, excitement, and motivational potential must be experienced to be appreciated.

REFERENCES AND READINGS

Davidson, R. J., & Schwartz, G. E. Brain Mechanisms Specificity and Pattern-ing. *Psychophysiology*, November 1977, pp. 598-601.

Desoille, R. The Directed Daydream. *The Psychosynthesis Research Founda-tion*, 1965, *8*, (Monograph)

Dubois, N. F., & Alverson, G. F., & Staley, R. K. *Educational Psychology and Instructional Decisions*. Homewood: The Dorsey Press, 1979.

Ellenberger, H. F. *The Discovery of the Unconscious.* New York: Basic Books, 1970.

Gold, S. R., & Cundiff, G. Increasing Frequency of Daydreaming. *Journal of Clinical Psychology*, 1980, 116-120.

Goodman, D. S., & Maultsby, M. C. *Emotional Well-Being Through Rational Behavior Training*, Springfield: Thomas, 1978.

Hamrick, M. H., Anspaugh, D. J., & Smith, D. L. Decision-making and the Behavior Gap. *Journal of School Health*, 1980, *50* (8), 455-458.

Jacobson, E. *Progressive Relaxation: A Physiological and Clinical Investiga-tion of Muscular States and Their Significance in Psychology and Medical Practice.* Chicago: University of Chicago Press, 1977.

Janis, I. L., & Mann, L. *Decision Making: A Psychological Analysis of Con-flict, Choice, and Commitment.* The Free Press, 1977.

Jung, C. G. *Memories, Dreams, Reflections,* New York: Pantheon Books, 1961.

Kentucky Department of Education. *Making Decisions: Alcohol and Drug Education Guide K-12.* pp. 65, 1976.

King, D. L. *Conditioning: An Image Approach,* New York: Garden Press, 1979.

Kroger, W. S., & Fezler, W. D. *Hypnosis and Behavior Modification: Imagery Conditioning.* Philadelphia: J. B. Lippincott, 1976.

Laing, R. D. *The Divided Self.* Chicago: Quadrangle Books, 1962.

Laing, R. D., Phillipson, H., & Lee, A. R. *Interpersonal Perception.* New York: Springer, 1966.

Lazarus, A. *In the Mind's Eye.* New York: Rawson Associates Publishers, Inc., 1977.

187

Maddi, S. The Search for Meaning. *Nebraska Symposium on Motivation.* Lincoln: University of Nebraska Press, 1970.

Maultsby, M. C. Rational Emotive Imagery. *Rational Living,* 1971, *6* (1), 24-26.

Maultsby, M. C. *A Million Dollars for Your Hangover.* Lexington: Rational Self Help Books, 1978.

Pearce, J. Values Education: Extending the View. *Journal of School Health,* 1979, 169-173.

Raths, L. E., Harmin, M., & Simon, S. *Values and Teaching,* Columbus: Charles E. Merrill Book, Inc., 1966.

Read, D. A., Simon, S. B., & Goodman, J. B. *Health Education: The Search for Values,* Englewood Cliffs: Prentice-Hall, Inc., 1977.

Richardson, A. Mental Practice: A Review and Discussion. *The Research Quarterly,* January 1967, pp. 95-107.

Richardson, A. Mental Practice: A Review and Discussion. *The Research Quarterly,* March 1967, pp. 263-273.

Richardson, G. E. The Life After Death Phenomenon. *Journal of School Health,* 1979, *49* (8), 451-453.

Richardson, G. E., & Jordan, R. Strategies for Creative Emergence. *Health Education,* 1981, *12* (1), 14-16.

Richardson, G. E., Educational Imagery: A Missing Link in Decision Making, *Journal of School Health,* 1981, *51*(8), 560-564.

Richardson, J. T. E. *Mental Imagery and Human Memory.* New York: St. Martin's Press, 1980.

Shaver, J. P., Strong, W. *Facing Value Decisions: Rationale-Building for Teachers,* Belmont: Wadsworth Publishing Co., 1976.

Shorr, J. E. *Imagery: Its Many Dimensions and Applications.* New York: Plenum Press, 1980.

Shorr, J. E. *Psychotherapy through Imagery.* New York: Intercontinental Medical Book Corporation, 1974.

Simon, S. B., Howe, L. W., & Kirshenbawn, H. *Values Clarification, A Handbook of Practical Strategies for Teachers and Students,* New York: Hart Publishing Co., Inc.

Singer, J. L., & Switzer, E. *Mind Play — The Creative Use of Fantasy.* Englewood Cliffs: Prentice-Hall, 1980.

Sommer, R. *The Mind's Eye.* New York: Dell Publishing Co., 1978.

Stampfl, T. G. Essentials of Implosive Therapy: A Learning Theory Based on Psycho-Dynamic Behavioral Therapy. *Journal of Abnormal Psychology,* 1967, (72), 496-503.

Wolpe, J. *The Practice of Behavior Therapy.* New York: Pergamon Press, 1969.

INDEX